THE AVIATION WORKSHOP PUBLIC
ON TARGET PROFILE NO:

The English Electric/BAC ___
Part One: Featuring the B.2, B.6, B.15, B.16, E.15, PR.3, PR.7, T.4, T.17, T.19 and TT.18, in RAF and FAA service
by Jon Freeman

The prototype of the English Electric A-1 jet-engined medium bomber, took to the air on Friday, 13 May 1949. Entering RAF service during the spring of 1951, few people then could have possibly imagined that over 50 years later, the Canberra would still be in operational use with the RAF. From its origins as a medium bomber, the Canberra undertook high-altitude reconnaissance roles, ECM training, target-towing and other specialist work, with the basic airframe remaining essentially the same, apart from improved engines and additional lumps, bumps and excrescences for specialist roles, establishing the aircraft as an outstandingly versatile and reliable design.

'Part One' of this two-part tribute to one of 'Britain's Best', features the colour schemes and markings of the 'bubble canopy' variants in RAF and FAA service, from the initial Medium Altitude Night Bomber Scheme of Medium Sea Grey over Anti-Searchlight Glossy Black to the current Camouflage Grey (Hemp) over Light Aircraft Grey scheme.

The unit markings are numerous, often with several variations to them. We have included as many as we could find in the eighty-four profiles and twenty-one four-views - including RAF Station markings such as Honington's 'Pheasant', Cottesmore's 'Horseshoe' and Akrotiri's 'Flamingo'. No doubt we have missed some, but if our ongoing research uncovers any more, these will be included in **'EE Canberra: Part Two'**, which will primarily cover the RAF's B(I)8 and PR.9 variants and the Canberra's worldwide overseas operators.

Publisher's Note
In preparing this book, we have worked exclusively from photographs, either in published reference books or from privately loaned sources. Great care has been taken to cross-reference all available data and research material sources where possible and to this end five books need special mention - *'English Electric Canberra'* by Ken Delve, Peter Green and John Clemons, Midland Counties Publications, 1992; *'English Electric Canberra'* by Roland Beamont and Arthur Reed, Ian Allan Ltd, 1984; *Canberra - the Operational Record'* by Robert Jackson, Airlife, 1988; *'English Electric Canberra and Martin B-57'* by Barry Jones, Crowood Press, 1999; and *'Bomber Squadrons of the RAF'* by Philip J R Moyes, MacDonald & Co Ltd, 1964. Grateful thanks are also due to Dale Clarke, Mike McEvoy and Martin Blundell.
Neil Robinson
Series Editor
June 2005

First Published in Great Britain in 2005
by The Aviation Workshop Publications Ltd.,
'Mapledene', 13 Charlton Road, Wantage, Oxfordshire, OX12 8EP, UK
Tel: 01235 769038. Fax: 01235 769746
E-mail: aviation-workshop@btconnect.com
Website: www.theaviationworkshop.co.uk

Edited by Neil Robinson
Artwork by Jon Freeman
Designed by AIRgen Publications Ltd
Printed in the UK by PHP Litho Printers Ltd
Hoyle Mill, Barnsley, South Yorkshire S71 1HN
ISBN 1-904643-25-6

Canberra B.2
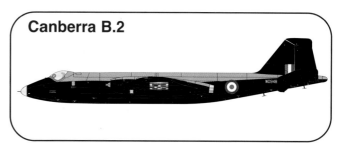

Canberra PR.3
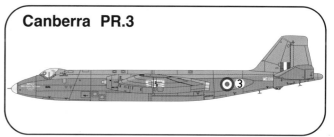

Canberra T.4
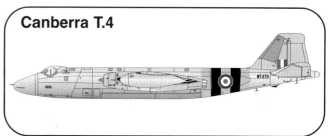

Canberra PR.7
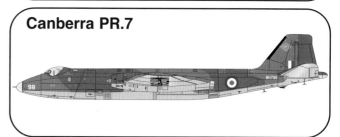

Canberra B.16
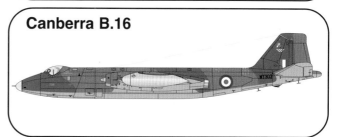

Canberra TT.18
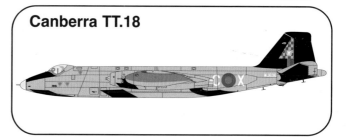

English Electric B3/45 prototype A1 (Canberra), VN799, Warton, May 1949
The initial Canberra prototype, VN799, as it looked prior to its maiden flight in the hands of Roland P Beamont, English Electric's Chief Test Pilot and distinguished World War Two fighter pilot, at Warton on 13 May 1949. At this point, the Canberra was still referred to as the English Electric A1. Finished in the distinctive overall 'Petter Blue', paint scheme, (named after the aircraft's designer, W E W 'Teddy' Petter), VN799 carried no upper or under wing roundels at this time, just the serial number in white under the wings and on either side of the fuselage, together with the prototype 'P' marking. Note the original rudder top profile, dorsal fin strake and the fully glazed canopy without the solid rear fairing.
References used: pp15 to 23, 'English Electric Canberra' by Roland Beamont and Arthur Reed, Ian Allan Ltd, 1984

English Electric B3/45 prototype A1 (Canberra), VN799, Warton, June 1949
Following modifications to the rudder top, VN799, continued its development trials throughout the summer of 1949 and made an appearance at the SBAC Show at Farnborough in September, still in the highly polished overall 'Petter Blue', paint scheme. VN799 was still bereft of upper or under wing roundels, and just carried the serial number in white under the wings and on either side of the fuselage, together with the prototype 'P' marking. Note the shape of the modified rudder top profile, retention of the dorsal fin strake and the fully glazed canopy, still without the solid rear fairing.

References used: pp25 and 26, 'English Electric Canberra' by Roland Beamont and Arthur Reed, Ian Allan Ltd, 1984

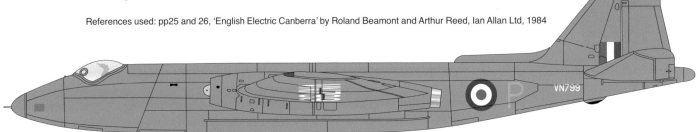

English Electric B.1, third prototype Canberra, VN828, Warton, November 1949
Following further modifications to the design, including the deletion of the dorsal fin strake, the third prototype, VN828 was finished in the Medium Altitude Night Bomber Scheme of Medium Sea Grey upper surfaces over Anti-Searchlight Glossy Black under surfaces to Pattern No 2. Roundels were carried above the wings and on the fuselage sides, with just the serial number, in white, under the wings, and on the fuselage sides. Note the Prototype 'P' marking to the rear of the fuselage roundel, and the canopy, still without the solid rear fairing.

References used: p39, 'English Electric Canberra' by Roland Beamont and Arthur Reed, Ian Allan Ltd, 1984

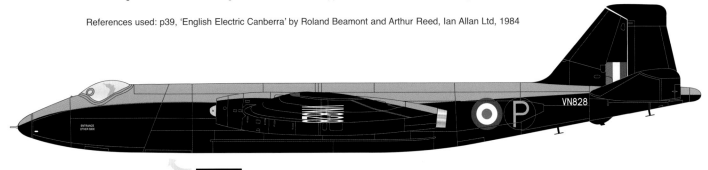

English Electric Canberra B.2, WD980, of No 617 Sqn, RAF Binbrook, February 1952
WD980 was one of the last Canberra B.2s to be finished in the Medium Altitude Night Bomber Scheme of Medium Sea Grey upper surfaces over Anti-Searchlight Glossy Black under surfaces to Pattern No 2. Roundels were carried above the wings and on the fuselage sides, with the serial number, in white, under the wings and on the rear fuselage sides. The red Binbrook Station 'lightning flash' denotes No 617 Squadron. Note that the canopy is fitted with the production solid rear fairing.
References used: p25, 'English Electric Canberra' by Ken Delve, Peter Green and John Clemons, Midland Counties Publications, 1992 References used: p39, 'English Electric Canberra' by Roland Beamont and Arthur Reed, Ian Allan Ltd, 1984

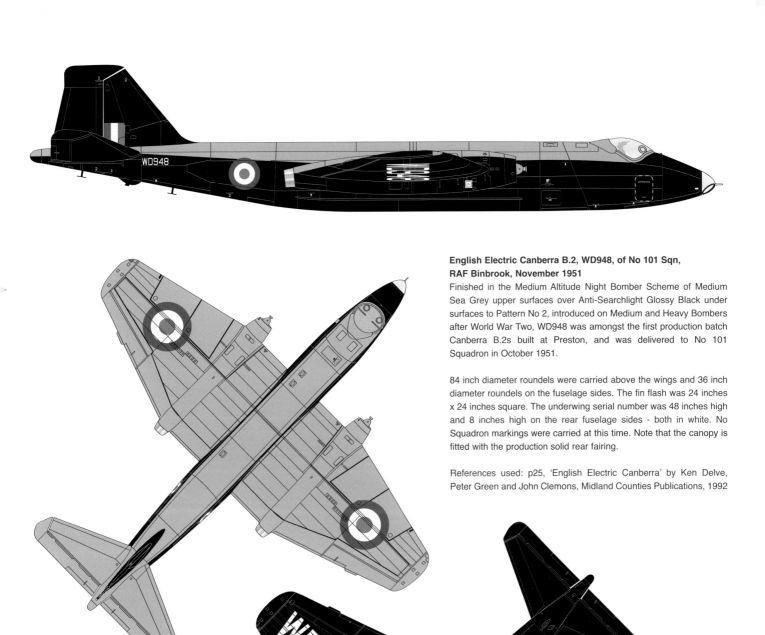

English Electric Canberra B.2, WD948, of No 101 Sqn, RAF Binbrook, November 1951

Finished in the Medium Altitude Night Bomber Scheme of Medium Sea Grey upper surfaces over Anti-Searchlight Glossy Black under surfaces to Pattern No 2, introduced on Medium and Heavy Bombers after World War Two, WD948 was amongst the first production batch Canberra B.2s built at Preston, and was delivered to No 101 Squadron in October 1951.

84 inch diameter roundels were carried above the wings and 36 inch diameter roundels on the fuselage sides. The fin flash was 24 inches x 24 inches square. The underwing serial number was 48 inches high and 8 inches high on the rear fuselage sides - both in white. No Squadron markings were carried at this time. Note that the canopy is fitted with the production solid rear fairing.

References used: p25, 'English Electric Canberra' by Ken Delve, Peter Green and John Clemons, Midland Counties Publications, 1992

English Electric Canberra B.2, WP515, of No 231 OCU, RAF Bassingbourn, circa 1957

WP515 was one of two replacement B.2s, (the other being WP514), to cover two airframes, (WD939 and WD983), that had been diverted off-contract. Delivered to No 12 Sqn in March 1952, WP515 also served with No 617 Sqn before joining 231 OCU. Finished in the Medium Altitude Night Bomber Scheme of Medium Sea Grey upper surfaces over Anti-Searchlight Glossy Black under surfaces to Pattern No 2, roundels were carried above the wings and on the fuselage sides, with the serial number, in white, under the wings and on the rear fuselage sides. Note that the Aluminium painted wing tip drop tanks that were carried during its service with 231 OCU circa 1957.

References used: p251, 'English Electric Canberra' by Ken Delve, Peter Green and John Clemons, Midland Counties Publications, 1992

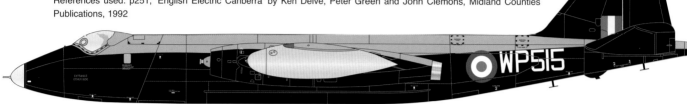

English Electric Canberra B.2, WD994, of No 12 Sqn, RAF Binbrook, autumn 1952

WD999 was amongst the first airframes of the first production batch to be finished in the High Altitude Day Bomber Scheme of Medium Sea Grey and Light Slate Grey upper surfaces with PRU Blue undersides to Pattern No 2, and served with No 12 Sqn until it crashed in November 1952. Roundels were carried above the wings and on the fuselage sides, with the serial number, in white, under the wings and on the rear fuselage sides. Note the gold No 12 Sqn 'Binbrook Station' lightning flash on the nose.

Inset: No 12 Squadron's badge.

References used: Private photo archives

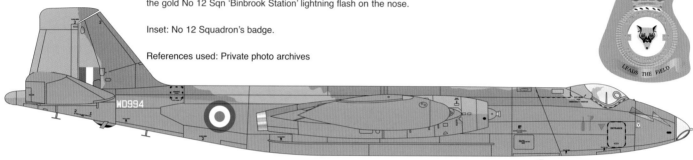

English Electric Canberra PR.3, WE141, of No 540 Sqn, RAF Benson, spring 1953

From the first production batch of twenty-seven Canberra PR.3s, WE141 was finished in the then standard High Altitude Photo Reconnaissance Scheme of Medium Sea Grey upper surfaces with PRU Blue undersides to Pattern No 2. Roundels were carried above the wings and on the fuselage sides, with the serial number, in white, under the wings and on the rear fuselage sides.

References used: p30, 'English Electric Canberra' by Ken Delve, Peter Green and John Clemons, Midland Counties Publications, 1992

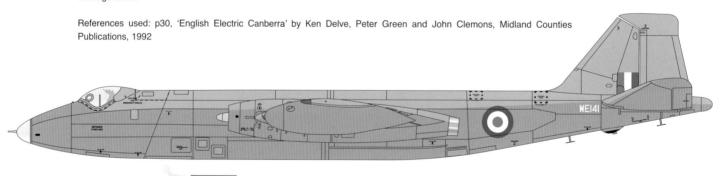

English Electric Canberra B.2, WJ616, of No 199 Sqn, RAF Hemswell, on detachment to Habbaniya, Iraq, circa 1954

A Handley Page built B.2, WJ616 was completed on the production line, finished in the new overall High Speed Silver scheme introduced at the end of 1952. Roundels were carried above the wings and on the fuselage sides, with the serial number, in black, under the wings and on the rear fuselage sides. Note the yellow and black Hemswell Station 'flash' on the fin.

References used: p48, 'English Electric Canberra' by Ken Delve, Peter Green and John Clemons, Midland Counties Publications, 1992

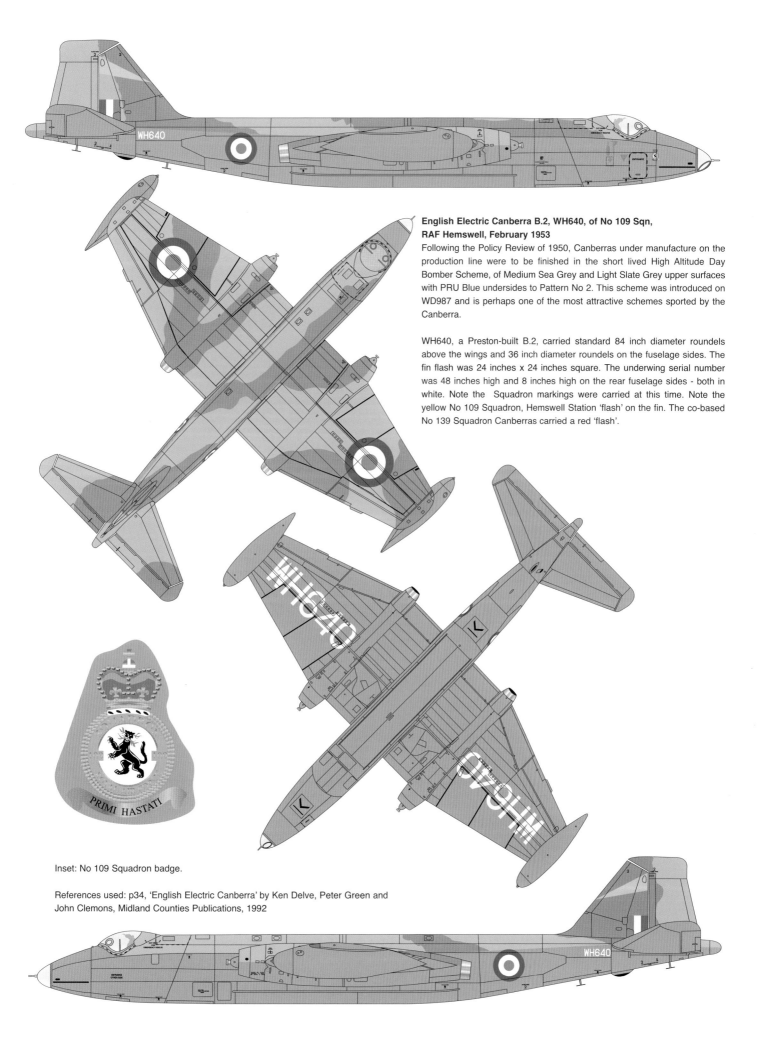

English Electric Canberra B.2, WH640, of No 109 Sqn, RAF Hemswell, February 1953

Following the Policy Review of 1950, Canberras under manufacture on the production line were to be finished in the short lived High Altitude Day Bomber Scheme, of Medium Sea Grey and Light Slate Grey upper surfaces with PRU Blue undersides to Pattern No 2. This scheme was introduced on WD987 and is perhaps one of the most attractive schemes sported by the Canberra.

WH640, a Preston-built B.2, carried standard 84 inch diameter roundels above the wings and 36 inch diameter roundels on the fuselage sides. The fin flash was 24 inches x 24 inches square. The underwing serial number was 48 inches high and 8 inches high on the rear fuselage sides - both in white. Note the Squadron markings were carried at this time. Note the yellow No 109 Squadron, Hemswell Station 'flash' on the fin. The co-based No 139 Squadron Canberras carried a red 'flash'.

Inset: No 109 Squadron badge.

References used: p34, 'English Electric Canberra' by Ken Delve, Peter Green and John Clemons, Midland Counties Publications, 1992

English Electric Canberra B.6, WJ768, of No 109 Sqn, RAF Hemswell, circa 1954
During the summer of 1954 an improved variant of the Canberra B.2, the B.6, was starting to put in an appearance. One of the first squadrons to change over to the B.6 was No 109 Sqn, and WJ768, was one of the first Canberra B.6s built, by English Electric at Preston. It was finished in the overall High Speed Silver scheme introduced at the end of 1952. Roundels were carried above the wings and on the fuselage sides, with the serial number, in black, under the wings and on the rear fuselage sides. Note the yellow with black trim, No 109 Sqn, Hemswell Station 'flash' on the fin.
Inset: No 109 Squadron badge.
References used: p3378 'RAF Squadrons' partwork

English Electric Canberra B.2, WJ641, of No 50 Sqn, RAF Upwood, early 1956
Having previously served with Nos 109 and 40 Squadrons, this Handley Page built B.2, WJ641 was passed on to No 50 Sqn and served with the unit when it was stationed at RAF Upwood in Huntingdonshire during the mid/late 1950s. Finished in the overall High Speed Silver scheme, roundels were carried above the wings and on the fuselage sides, with the serial number, in black, under the wings and on the rear fuselage sides - in the 'squared-off' style. Note the yellow Upwood Station 'shield and rampant lion' on the fin and the No 50 Squadron 'sword' marking on the tip tanks.

References used: p78 'Bomber Squadrons of the RAF' by Philip J R Moyes, MacDonald & Co Ltd, 1964 (Third impression 1971), and p247, 'English Electric Canberra' by Ken Delve, Peter Green and John Clemons, Midland Counties Publications, 1992

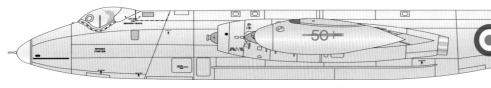

English Electric Canberra B.2, WH923, of No 61 Sqn, RAF Upwood, early 1956
The re-equipment of Bomber Command with Canberras continued throughout the mid-1950s, with the Wittering Wing, (Nos 61, 76 and 100 Squadrons), receiving the type. WH923 is illustrated here as she looked when stationed at RAF Upwood in Huntingdonshire during the mid/late 1950s. Finished in the overall High Speed Silver scheme, roundels were carried above the wings and on the fuselage sides, with the serial number, in black, under the wings and on the rear fuselage sides. Note the yellow Upwood Station 'shield and rampant lion' on the fin and the red 'Lincoln Imp' marking on the tip tanks.

References used: Private photo archives and p95 'Bomber Squadrons of the RAF' by Philip J R Moyes, MacDonald & Co Ltd, 1964 (Third impression 1971)

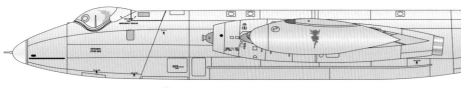

English Electric Canberra B.2, WJ609, of No 21 Sqn, on detachment to Khormaksar, Aden, March 1955
Reformed at RAF Scampton in September 1953, No 21 Sqn sent a detachment of four aircraft, including WJ609 illustrated here, on a goodwill tour of the Middle East in March 1955. Finished in the overall High Speed Silver scheme, roundels were carried above the wings and on the fuselage sides, with the serial number, in black, under the wings and on the rear fuselage sides. Note the red No 21 Sqn 'XXI' crossed keys and squadron badge on the nose. See insets for enlargements.

References used: p43, 'English Electric Canberra' by Ken Delve, Peter Green and John Clemons, Midland Counties Publications, 1992

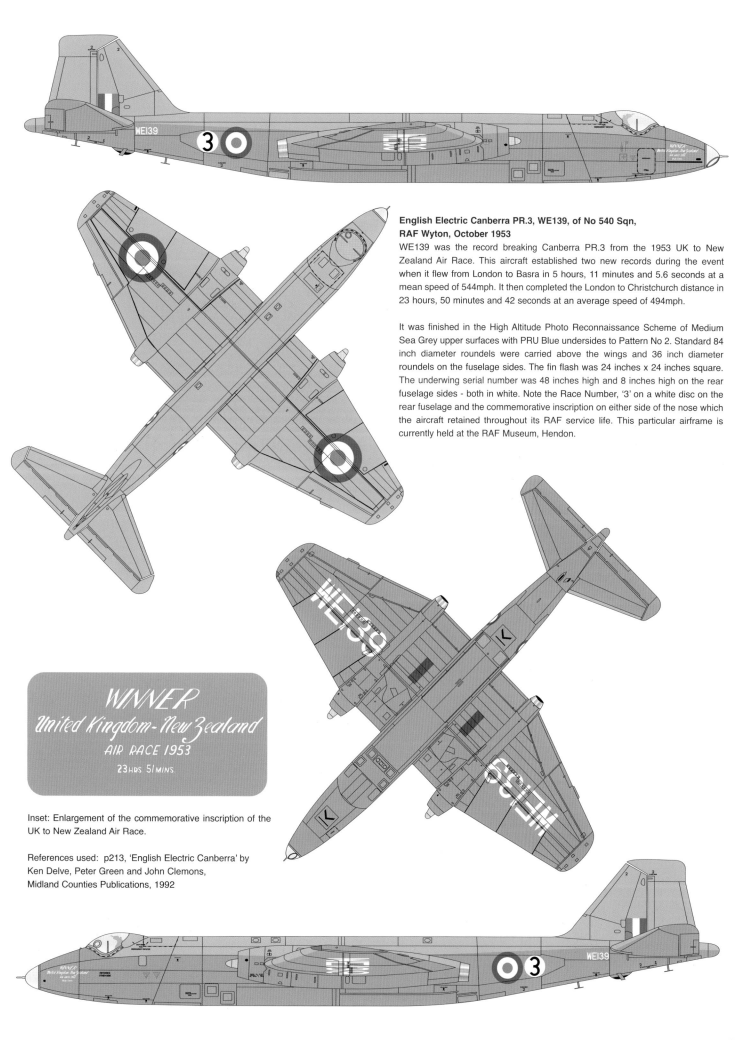

English Electric Canberra PR.3, WE139, of No 540 Sqn, RAF Wyton, October 1953

WE139 was the record breaking Canberra PR.3 from the 1953 UK to New Zealand Air Race. This aircraft established two new records during the event when it flew from London to Basra in 5 hours, 11 minutes and 5.6 seconds at a mean speed of 544mph. It then completed the London to Christchurch distance in 23 hours, 50 minutes and 42 seconds at an average speed of 494mph.

It was finished in the High Altitude Photo Reconnaissance Scheme of Medium Sea Grey upper surfaces with PRU Blue undersides to Pattern No 2. Standard 84 inch diameter roundels were carried above the wings and 36 inch diameter roundels on the fuselage sides. The fin flash was 24 inches x 24 inches square. The underwing serial number was 48 inches high and 8 inches high on the rear fuselage sides - both in white. Note the Race Number, '3' on a white disc on the rear fuselage and the commemorative inscription on either side of the nose which the aircraft retained throughout its RAF service life. This particular airframe is currently held at the RAF Museum, Hendon.

WINNER
United Kingdom-New Zealand
AIR RACE 1953
23 HRS. 51 MINS.

Inset: Enlargement of the commemorative inscription of the UK to New Zealand Air Race.

References used: p213, 'English Electric Canberra' by Ken Delve, Peter Green and John Clemons, Midland Counties Publications, 1992

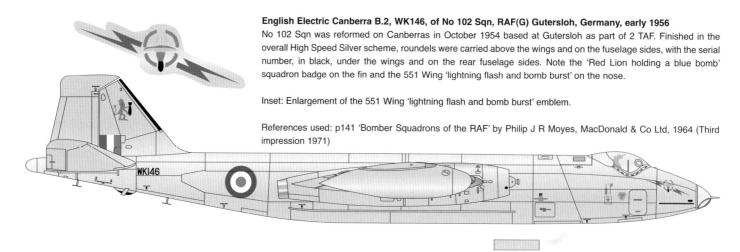

English Electric Canberra B.2, WK146, of No 102 Sqn, RAF(G) Gutersloh, Germany, early 1956
No 102 Sqn was reformed on Canberras in October 1954 based at Gutersloh as part of 2 TAF. Finished in the overall High Speed Silver scheme, roundels were carried above the wings and on the fuselage sides, with the serial number, in black, under the wings and on the rear fuselage sides. Note the 'Red Lion holding a blue bomb' squadron badge on the fin and the 551 Wing 'lightning flash and bomb burst' on the nose.

Inset: Enlargement of the 551 Wing 'lightning flash and bomb burst' emblem.

References used: p141 'Bomber Squadrons of the RAF' by Philip J R Moyes, MacDonald & Co Ltd, 1964 (Third impression 1971)

English Electric Canberra B.2, WK130, of No 35 Sqn, RAF Marham, 1955
No 35 Sqn replaced its Boeing Washingtons with Canberra B.2s in April 1954. Finished in the overall High Speed Silver scheme, roundels were carried above the wings and on the fuselage sides, with the serial number, in black, under the wings and on the rear fuselage sides, repeated on the nosewheel doors. Note the 35 Sqn 'Winged Horse' shield and red lightning flash on the fin which was repeated on the wing tip tanks.

Inset: Enlargement of the 35 Sqn 'Winged Horse' shield and yellow lightning flash.

References used: p38, 'English Electric Canberra' by Ken Delve, Peter Green and John Clemons, Midland Counties Publications, 1992

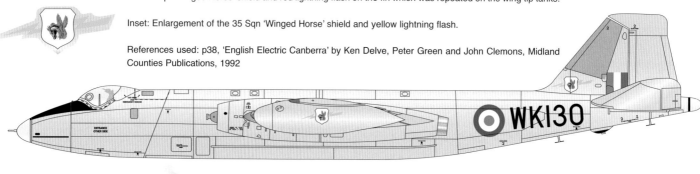

English Electric Canberra B.2, WJ733, of No 18 Sqn, RAF Upwood, summer 1955
WJ733 is illustrated as it looked for the visit to RAF Upwood by the Sultan of Muscat and Oman, in July 1955. Finished in the overall High Speed Silver scheme, roundels were carried above the wings and on the fuselage sides, with the serial number, in black, under the wings and on the rear fuselage sides. Note the 18 Sqn 'Prancing Horse' on the wing tip tanks.

Inset: Enlargement of the 18 Sqn 'Prancing Horse'.
References used: p37, 'English Electric Canberra' by Ken Delve, Peter Green and John Clemons, Midland Counties Publications, 1992

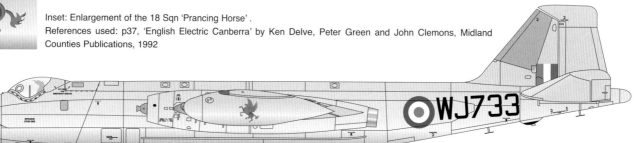

English Electric Canberra B.6, WT371, of No 139 Sqn, RAF Hemswell, August 1955
Named the 'Jamaica Squadron', due to a fund to buy bombers by a Jamaican newspaper during World War Two, No 139 Sqn made a goodwill visit to the Caribbean, as part of the Colony's Tercentenary Celebrations, in the summer of 1955. WT371 is illustrated as it looked immediately prior the visit, finished in the overall High Speed Silver scheme. Standard roundels were carried above the wings and on the fuselage sides, with the serial number, in black, under the wings and on the rear fuselage sides. Note the red and white Hemswell Station 'flash' on the fin and the No 139 (Jamaica) Sqn badge on the nose.

Inset: No 139 (Jamaica) Sqn badge.
References used: p43, 'English Electric Canberra' by Ken Delve, Peter Green and John Clemons, Midland Counties Publications, 1992

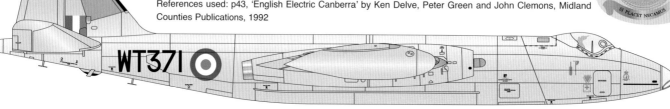

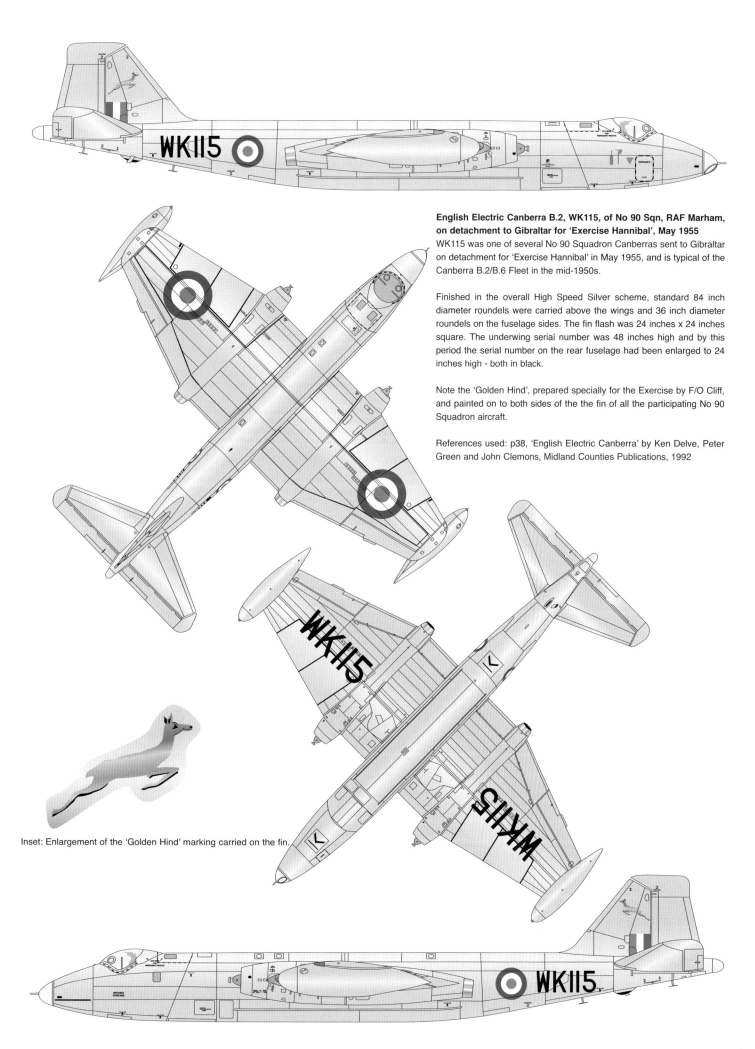

English Electric Canberra B.2, WK115, of No 90 Sqn, RAF Marham, on detachment to Gibraltar for 'Exercise Hannibal', May 1955

WK115 was one of several No 90 Squadron Canberras sent to Gibraltar on detachment for 'Exercise Hannibal' in May 1955, and is typical of the Canberra B.2/B.6 Fleet in the mid-1950s.

Finished in the overall High Speed Silver scheme, standard 84 inch diameter roundels were carried above the wings and 36 inch diameter roundels on the fuselage sides. The fin flash was 24 inches x 24 inches square. The underwing serial number was 48 inches high and by this period the serial number on the rear fuselage had been enlarged to 24 inches high - both in black.

Note the 'Golden Hind', prepared specially for the Exercise by F/O Cliff, and painted on to both sides of the the fin of all the participating No 90 Squadron aircraft.

References used: p38, 'English Electric Canberra' by Ken Delve, Peter Green and John Clemons, Midland Counties Publications, 1992

Inset: Enlargement of the 'Golden Hind' marking carried on the fin.

English Electric Canberra B.2, WD995, of No 103 Sqn, RAF(G), Gutersloh, Germany, June 1955
No 103 Sqn spent a relatively brief time on Canberras, with 2 TAF, RAF Germany, re-forming on the type in November 1954 only to be disbanded again at the end of July 1956. WD995 was finished in the High Altitude Day Bomber Scheme of Medium Sea Grey and Light Slate Grey upper surfaces with PRU Blue undersides to Pattern No 2. Roundels were carried above the wings and on the fuselage sides, with the serial number, in white, under the wings and on the rear fuselage sides. No squadron or station markings appear to have been carried.

Inset: No 103 Squadron's badge.
References used: p238, 'English Electric Canberra' by Ken Delve, Peter Green and John Clemons, Midland Counties Publications, 1992

English Electric Canberra B.6, WH977, of No 9 Sqn, RAF Coningsby, January 1956
Finished in the overall High Speed Silver scheme, WH977 was regularly flown by No 9 Squadron's CO, W/Cdr L G Bastard. Roundels were carried above the wings and on the fuselage sides, with the serial number, in black, under the wings and on the rear fuselage sides. Note the No 9 Sqn blue 'Lightning Flash' on the nose.

References used: p46, 'English Electric Canberra' by Ken Delve, Peter Green and John Clemons, Midland Counties Publications, 1992; and p24 'Canberra - the Operational Record' by Robert Jackson , Airlife, 1988

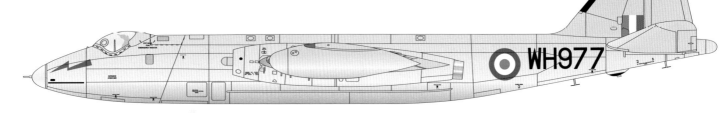

English Electric Canberra B.2, WJ628, of No 104 Sqn, RAF(G) Gutersloh, Germany, February 1956
Equipping another of the 'short-lived' RAF Germany Canberra squadrons, from March 1955 to July 1956, WJ628 was finished in the overall High Speed Silver scheme. Roundels were carried above the wings and on the fuselage sides, with the serial number, in black, under the wings and on the rear fuselage sides. Note the No 104 Sqn 'Thunderbolt' on the fin and the squadron badge on the nose.

Inset: Enlargements of No 104 Squadron's 'Thunderbolt' on the fin (left) and the squadron badge on the nose (right).

References used: p247, 'English Electric Canberra' by Ken Delve, Peter Green and John Clemons, Midland Counties Publications, 1992

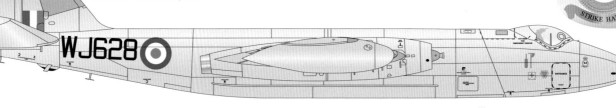

English Electric Canberra B.2, WT713, of No 149 Sqn, RAF(G) Gutersloh, Germany, July 1956
In August 1954, No 149 Sqn became the first Canberra squadron to be permanently based in Germany, as part of 2 TAF. The squadron was disbanded in August 1956. WT713 was finished in the standard overall High Speed Silver scheme. Roundels were carried above the wings and on the fuselage sides, with the serial number, in black, under the wings and on the rear fuselage sides. Note the No 149 Sqn 'horseshoe and lightning flash' on the fin and the 551 Wing 'lightning flash and bomb burst' on the nose
Inset: Enlargements of No 149 Squadron's 'lightning flash and bomb burst' on the nose (right) and the squadron badge on the fin (left).
References used: p51, 'English Electric Canberra' by Ken Delve, Peter Green and John Clemons, Midland Counties Publications, 1992

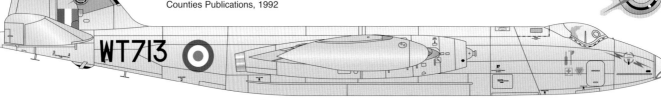

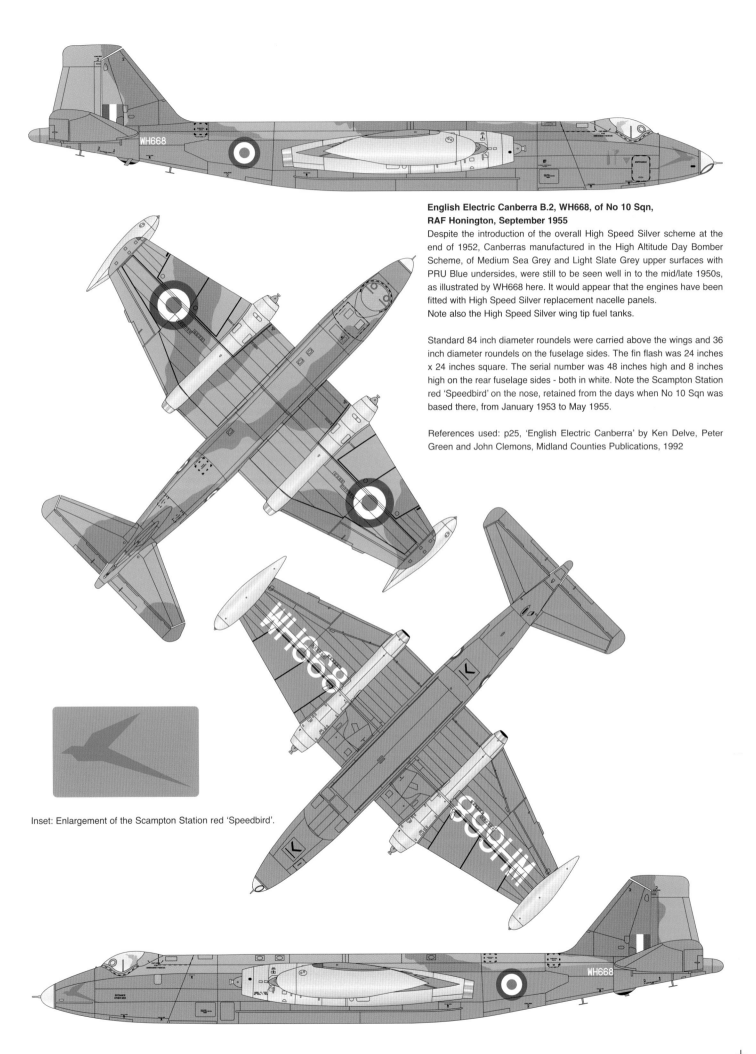

English Electric Canberra B.2, WH668, of No 10 Sqn, RAF Honington, September 1955

Despite the introduction of the overall High Speed Silver scheme at the end of 1952, Canberras manufactured in the High Altitude Day Bomber Scheme, of Medium Sea Grey and Light Slate Grey upper surfaces with PRU Blue undersides, were still to be seen well in to the mid/late 1950s, as illustrated by WH668 here. It would appear that the engines have been fitted with High Speed Silver replacement nacelle panels.
Note also the High Speed Silver wing tip fuel tanks.

Standard 84 inch diameter roundels were carried above the wings and 36 inch diameter roundels on the fuselage sides. The fin flash was 24 inches x 24 inches square. The serial number was 48 inches high and 8 inches high on the rear fuselage sides - both in white. Note the Scampton Station red 'Speedbird' on the nose, retained from the days when No 10 Sqn was based there, from January 1953 to May 1955.

References used: p25, 'English Electric Canberra' by Ken Delve, Peter Green and John Clemons, Midland Counties Publications, 1992

Inset: Enlargement of the Scampton Station red 'Speedbird'.

English Electric Canberra B.6, WH970, of No 12 Sqn, on detachment to Hal Far, Malta, for 'Operation Musketeer', Suez Crisis, autumn 1956

Equipped with the improved B.6 version, No 12 Squadron was one of five Canberra units, despatched from its UK home base, (of RAF Binbrook), to Malta in September 1956, for 'Operation Musketeer'. Finished in the overall High Speed Silver scheme, standard roundels were carried above the wings and on the fuselage sides. The underwing serial number and the enlarged to 24 inch high serial number on the rear fuselage were both black. Approximately 12 inch wide black and yellow 'Suez Stripes' were applied to the wings and the rear fuselage, those on the fuselage truncated around the roundel and serial number. Note the No 12 Sqn 'Red Fox' on the fin

Inset: Enlargement of the No 12 Sqn 'Red Fox' marking carried on the fin.

References used: p71, 'English Electric Canberra' by Ken Delve, Peter Green and John Clemons, Midland Counties Publications, 1992; and p30, 'Bomber Squadrons of the RAF' by Philip J R Moyes, MacDonald & Co Ltd, 1964 (Third Impression 1971)

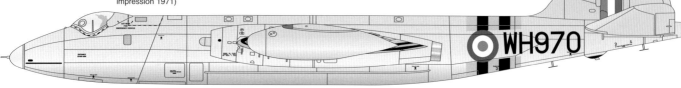

English Electric Canberra B.2, WH718, of No 44 Sqn, on detachment to RAF Nicosia, Cyprus, for 'Operation Musketeer', Suez Crisis, autumn 1956

No 44 was one of seven squadrons sent to Cyprus, (from its UK home base of RAF Honington), five of which still had Canberra B.2s, like No 44, whilst the others were equipped with the improved B.6 version. Finished in the overall High Speed Silver scheme, standard roundels were carried above the wings and on the fuselage sides. The underwing serial number and the enlarged to 24 inch high serial number on the rear fuselage were both black. Due to a lack of enough Yellow paint, black and 'cream', (mixed at unit level), 'Suez Stripes' were applied to the wings and the rear fuselage, those on the fuselage truncated around the roundel and serial number. Note the width of the 'Suez Stripes' - Cyprus-based Canberras often carried wider stripes than those on Malta-based Canberras, being approximately 24 inches wide. Note the 'Honington Pheasant' on the fin.

Inset: Enlargement of the 'Honington Pheasant' marking carried on the fin.

References used: Private photo archives

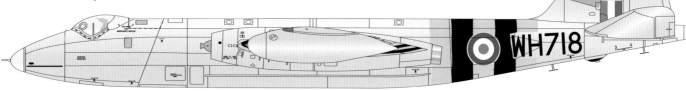

English Electric Canberra B.2, XA536, of No 15 Sqn, on detachment to RAF Nicosia, Cyprus, for 'Operation Musketeer', Suez Crisis, autumn 1956

One of the seven Bomber Command squadrons sent to Cyprus from its UK home base of RAF Honington, No 15 was still equipped with the Canberra B.2. XA536 illustrated here, was a replacement for B.2 WD991 which crashed before delivery and was finished in the overall High Speed Silver scheme. Standard roundels were carried above the wings and on the fuselage sides. The underwing serial number and the enlarged to 24 inch high serial number on the rear fuselage were both black. Black and 'cream', 'Suez Stripes' were applied to the wings and the rear fuselage, those on the fuselage painted around the roundel and serial number. Note the 24 inch wide 'Suez Stripes' - carried by Cyprus-based Canberras - and the 'Honington Pheasant' on the fin.

Inset: Enlargement of the 'Honington Pheasant' marking carried on the fin.

References used: p73, 'English Electric Canberra' by Ken Delve, Peter Green and John Clemons, Midland Counties Publications, 1992

English Electric Canberra PR.7, WH801, of No 13 Sqn, on detachment to RAF Akrotiri, Cyprus, for 'Operation Musketeer', Suez Crisis, autumn 1956

To provide reconnaissance support for 'Operation Musketeer', the RAF called in the Egypt-based Canberra PR.7s of No 13 Sqn. The Canberra PR.7 combined the airframe of the earlier PR.3 with new engines, anti-skid brakes and leading-edge fuel cells. Despite being a dedicated Photo Reconnaissance variant, WH801 was still finished in the overall High Speed Silver scheme, with standard roundels carried above the wings and on the fuselage sides. The serial number under the wings and on the rear fuselage were both in black, with the 'last three' repeated on the nosewheel doors. Approximately 24 inch wide black and 'cream' 'Suez Stripes' were applied to the wings and the rear fuselage, those on the fuselage were painted around the roundel but completely over the serial number.

References used: Private photo archives

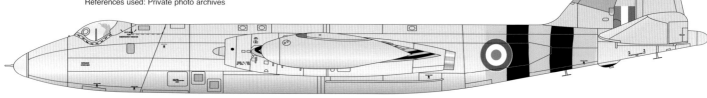

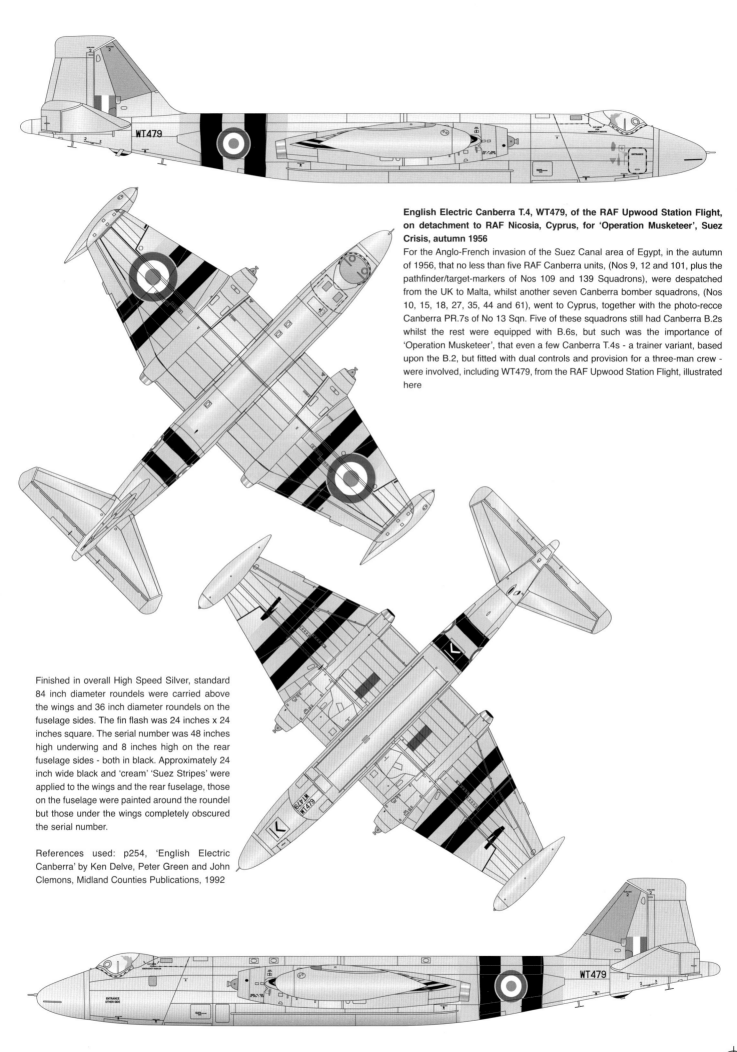

English Electric Canberra T.4, WT479, of the RAF Upwood Station Flight, on detachment to RAF Nicosia, Cyprus, for 'Operation Musketeer', Suez Crisis, autumn 1956

For the Anglo-French invasion of the Suez Canal area of Egypt, in the autumn of 1956, that no less than five RAF Canberra units, (Nos 9, 12 and 101, plus the pathfinder/target-markers of Nos 109 and 139 Squadrons), were despatched from the UK to Malta, whilst another seven Canberra bomber squadrons, (Nos 10, 15, 18, 27, 35, 44 and 61), went to Cyprus, together with the photo-recce Canberra PR.7s of No 13 Sqn. Five of these squadrons still had Canberra B.2s whilst the rest were equipped with B.6s, but such was the importance of 'Operation Musketeer', that even a few Canberra T.4s - a trainer variant, based upon the B.2, but fitted with dual controls and provision for a three-man crew - were involved, including WT479, from the RAF Upwood Station Flight, illustrated here

Finished in overall High Speed Silver, standard 84 inch diameter roundels were carried above the wings and 36 inch diameter roundels on the fuselage sides. The fin flash was 24 inches x 24 inches square. The serial number was 48 inches high underwing and 8 inches high on the rear fuselage sides - both in black. Approximately 24 inch wide black and 'cream' 'Suez Stripes' were applied to the wings and the rear fuselage, those on the fuselage were painted around the roundel but those under the wings completely obscured the serial number.

References used: p254, 'English Electric Canberra' by Ken Delve, Peter Green and John Clemons, Midland Counties Publications, 1992

English Electric Canberra B.2, WH729, of No 27 Sqn, on detachment to RAF Nicosia, Cyprus, for 'Operation Musketeer', Suez Crisis, autumn 1956

No 27 was another of the seven squadrons sent to Cyprus, (from its UK home base of RAF Waddington), for the Suez Crisis. Finished in the overall High Speed Silver scheme, standard roundels were carried above the wings and on the fuselage sides. The underwing and the rear fuselage serial number were both black. The lack of yellow paint, resulted in the 'Suez Stripes' being painted in black and 'cream', (mixed at unit level), which were applied, in approximately 24 inch wide bands, to the wings and the rear fuselage, those on the fuselage painted around the roundel. The City of Lincoln coat of arms, often carried by Waddington-based aircraft, was painted on the fin, with the 27 Sqn badge on the nose. Note the red lightning flash/cheatline applied to the full length of the fuselage, a feature of No 27 Sqn Canberras of this period.

Inset: Enlargement of the 'City of Lincoln' coat of arms carried on the fin and No 27 Squadron's badge on the nose.
References used: Private photo archives.

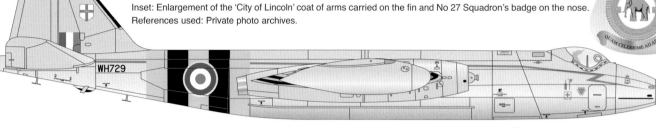

English Electric Canberra B.6, WH948, of No 101 Sqn, RAF Binbrook, September 1956

WH948 is illustrated as she looked on a visit to Blackbushe in September 1956, finished in the overall High Speed Silver scheme. Standard roundels were carried above the wings and on the fuselage sides, with the serial number, in black, under the wings and on the rear fuselage sides. Note the 101 Squadron black and white Binbrook Station 'flash' on the nose above the No 101 Sqn badge, which was repeated, in stylised form, on the fin.

Inset: No 101 Squadron's fin and nose badges.
References used: p38, 'English Electric Canberra' by Ken Delve, Peter Green and John Clemons, Midland Counties Publications, 1992

English Electric Canberra B.2, WJ630, of No 45 Sqn, RAF Tengah, Singapore, late 1957

No 45 Squadron collected its Canberra B.2s from Coningsby in November 1957 and flew them out to Tengah later the following month. As part of FEAF, the squadron saw action against terrorist insurgents in Malaya throughout 1958. WJ630 was finished in the overall High Speed Silver scheme with a black anti-glare panel on the nose. Standard roundels were carried above the wings and on the fuselage sides, with the serial number, in black, under the wings, on the rear fuselage and repeated on the nosewheel doors. The 45 Squadron 'Winged Camel' was carried on the fin.

References used: p96, 'English Electric Canberra' by Ken Delve, Peter Green and John Clemons, Midland Counties Publications, 1992

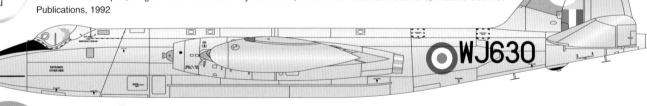

English Electric Canberra B.6, WH973, of No 9 Sqn, RAF Binbrook, on detachment to RAAF Butterworth, Malaya, March/April 1956

Another Canberra to see action over the Malayan jungle during the mid-1950s, WH973 was finished in the overall High Speed Silver scheme, with standard roundels above the wings and on the fuselage sides. The underwing and the rear fuselage serial number were both black. The No 9 Sqn 'Bat' marking was carried on the fin within a blue disc with the full squadron badge on the nose. Note the yellow 'Binbrook' lightning flash on the nose with the Union Flag underneath.

Inset: Enlargement of the 9 Squadron 'Bat' marking on the fin and No 9 Squadron's full badge on the nose.
References used: Private photo archives.

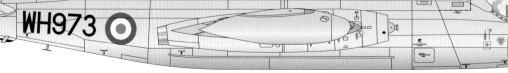

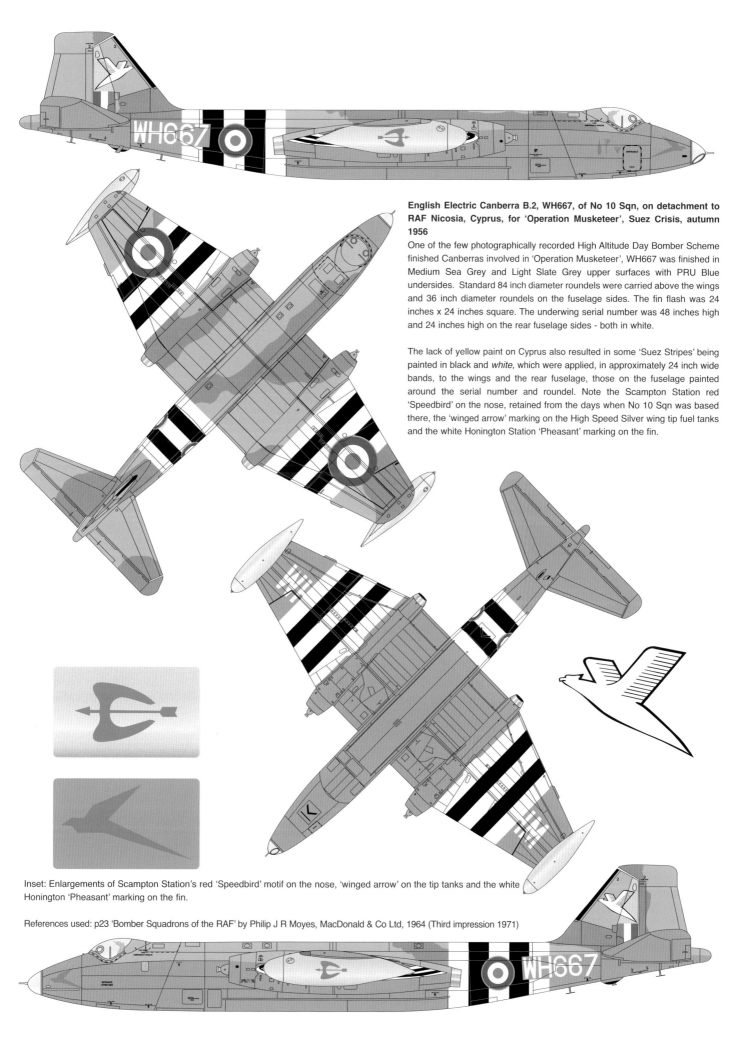

English Electric Canberra B.2, WH667, of No 10 Sqn, on detachment to RAF Nicosia, Cyprus, for 'Operation Musketeer', Suez Crisis, autumn 1956

One of the few photographically recorded High Altitude Day Bomber Scheme finished Canberras involved in 'Operation Musketeer', WH667 was finished in Medium Sea Grey and Light Slate Grey upper surfaces with PRU Blue undersides. Standard 84 inch diameter roundels were carried above the wings and 36 inch diameter roundels on the fuselage sides. The fin flash was 24 inches x 24 inches square. The underwing serial number was 48 inches high and 24 inches high on the rear fuselage sides - both in white.

The lack of yellow paint on Cyprus also resulted in some 'Suez Stripes' being painted in black and *white*, which were applied, in approximately 24 inch wide bands, to the wings and the rear fuselage, those on the fuselage painted around the serial number and roundel. Note the Scampton Station red 'Speedbird' on the nose, retained from the days when No 10 Sqn was based there, the 'winged arrow' marking on the High Speed Silver wing tip tanks and the white Honington Station 'Pheasant' marking on the fin.

Inset: Enlargements of Scampton Station's red 'Speedbird' motif on the nose, 'winged arrow' on the tip tanks and the white Honington 'Pheasant' marking on the fin.

References used: p23 'Bomber Squadrons of the RAF' by Philip J R Moyes, MacDonald & Co Ltd, 1964 (Third impression 1971)

English Electric Canberra B.2, WH638, of No 32 Sqn, RAF Weston Zoyland, January/February 1957

Previously a Middle East-based de Havilland Venom FB.1 unit, No 32 Squadron briefly returned to the UK during the winter of January/February 1957 to re-equip with Canberra B.2s, before re-deploying to Akrotiri, Cyprus in March 1957. WH638 is illustrated as she looked when undergoing crew familiarisation and training at Weston Zoyland, finished in the overall High Speed Silver scheme with a black anti-glare panel on the nose. Standard roundels were carried above the wings and on the fuselage sides. The underwing and the rear fuselage serial number were both black. Note the No 32 Squadron 'Blue and White' diagonal bar marking on the wooden section of the fin.

References used: p74, 'English Electric Canberra' by Ken Delve, Peter Green and John Clemons, Midland Counties Publications, 1992

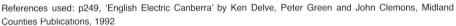

English Electric Canberra T.4, WJ880, of No 31 Sqn, RAF(G) Laarbruch, Germany, August 1958

Equipped with the Canberra PR.7 in March 1955, for the low-level photo recce role, No 31 Squadron also had a number of dual control, Canberra T.4 trainer variants on strength for pilot continuation training. WJ880, photographed at Bovingdon in August 1958, was finished in the overall High Speed Silver scheme, with 36 inch wide 'Trainer Bands' around the wings and rear fuselage. Standard roundels were carried above the wings and on the fuselage sides and the underwing and rear fuselage serial number were both black. Note the No 31 Squadron 'star' marking on the fin.

References used: p249, 'English Electric Canberra' by Ken Delve, Peter Green and John Clemons, Midland Counties Publications, 1992

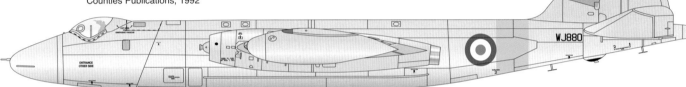

English Electric Canberra B.2, WK131, of No 57 Sqn, RAF Coningsby, summer 1957

No 57 Squadron spent most of June and July 1957 on detachment at Naples/Capodichino, Italy. WJ880, which was on the unit's strength at this time was finished in the standard overall High Speed Silver scheme, with standard roundels above the wings and on the fuselage sides. The underwing and rear fuselage serial number were both in black. Note the No 57 Squadron 'phoenix' marking in a shield on the fin.

Inset: Enlargement of the No 57 Sqn 'phoenix' marking on the fin.

References used: p38, 'English Electric Canberra' by Ken Delve, Peter Green and John Clemons, Midland Counties Publications, 1992; and p87, 'Bomber Squadrons of the RAF' by Philip J R Moyes, MacDonald & Co Ltd, 1964 (Third impression 1971)

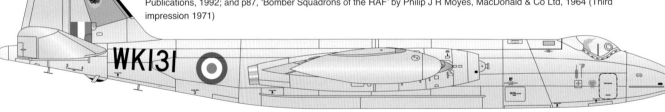

English Electric Canberra B.2, WH655, of No 249 Sqn, RAF Akrotiri, Cyprus, summer 1958

No 249 Squadron exchanged its Vampire FB.4s for Canberra B.2s, (and its role from fighter/ground attack to bomber), collecting its first Canberra aircraft from Coningsby in August 1957, and returning to Akrotiri with them. WH655, which was on the unit's strength in the summer of 1958, was finished in the standard overall High Speed Silver scheme, with standard roundels above the wings and on the fuselage sides. The underwing and rear fuselage serial number were both in black and the wing tip fuel tanks were yellow. Note the Akrotiri Wing 'pink flamingo' on the fin and the No 249 Squadron 'elephant' marking within a red 'spearhead' and black bar on the wing tip tanks.

Inset: Enlargements of the Akrotiri Wing 'pink flamingo' on the fin and the No 249 Squadron 'elephant' marking on the wing tip tanks.

References used: private photo archives

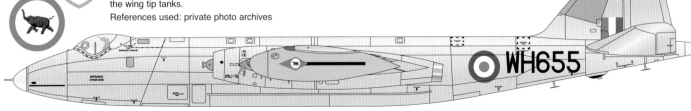

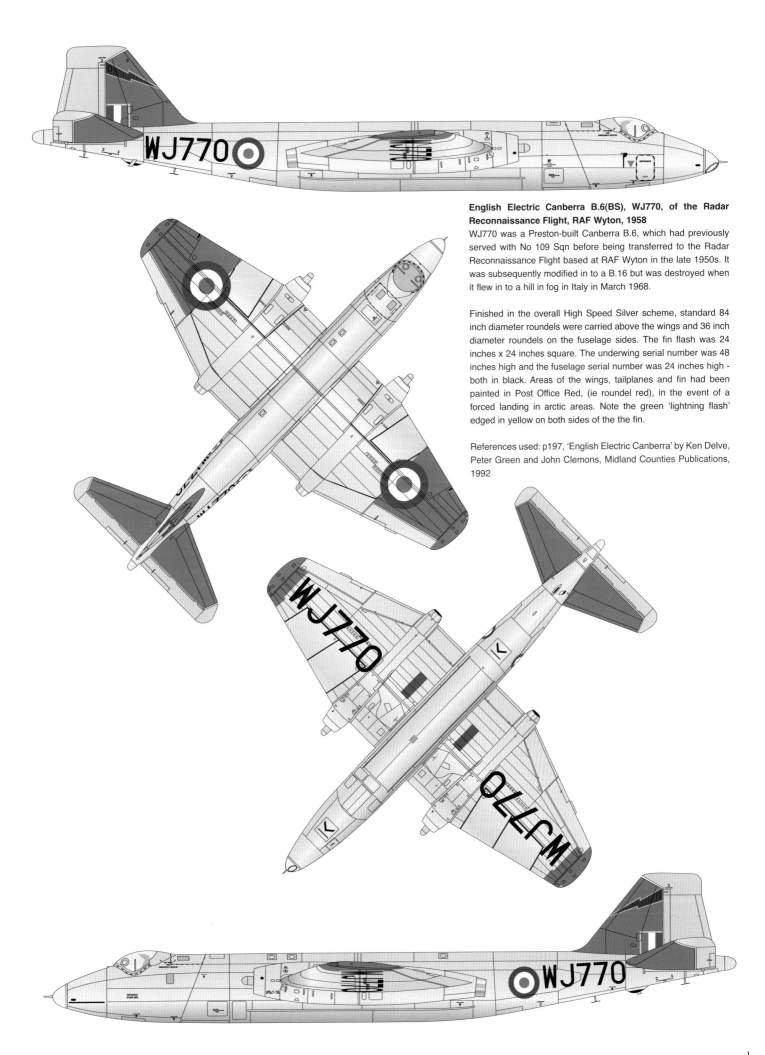

English Electric Canberra B.6(BS), WJ770, of the Radar Reconnaissance Flight, RAF Wyton, 1958

WJ770 was a Preston-built Canberra B.6, which had previously served with No 109 Sqn before being transferred to the Radar Reconnaissance Flight based at RAF Wyton in the late 1950s. It was subsequently modified in to a B.16 but was destroyed when it flew in to a hill in fog in Italy in March 1968.

Finished in the overall High Speed Silver scheme, standard 84 inch diameter roundels were carried above the wings and 36 inch diameter roundels on the fuselage sides. The fin flash was 24 inches x 24 inches square. The underwing serial number was 48 inches high and the fuselage serial number was 24 inches high - both in black. Areas of the wings, tailplanes and fin had been painted in Post Office Red, (ie roundel red), in the event of a forced landing in arctic areas. Note the green 'lightning flash' edged in yellow on both sides of the the fin.

References used: p197, 'English Electric Canberra' by Ken Delve, Peter Green and John Clemons, Midland Counties Publications, 1992

English Electric Canberra B.6, WH962, of No 76 Sqn, RAF Weston Zoyland, on detachment to Alice Springs, Australia, circa January/February 1957
WH962 is illustrated as she looked during the British nuclear weapons trials over Christmas Island during 1956/1957. The aircraft was specially painted in White Anti-flash Finish overall with pale grey and yellow special wing tip tanks fitted for atomic cloud sampling. Standard roundels were retained above the wings and on the fuselage sides. The underwing and the rear fuselage serial number were both black. Note No 76 Squadron's red 'lion guardant' marking on a white shield on the primer grey wooden section of the fin, and the red Kiwi 'zap' on the nose.

References used: p106, 'Bomber Squadrons of the RAF' by Philip J R Moyes, MacDonald & Co Ltd, 1964 (Third impression 1971); and p245 'English Electric Canberra' by Ken Delve, Peter Green and John Clemons, Midland Counties Publications, 1992

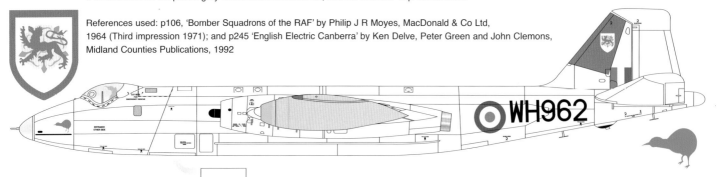

English Electric Canberra B.2, WK109, of No 6 Sqn, RAF Akrotiri, Cyprus, summer 1958
No 6 Squadron exchanged its Venom FB.4s for Canberra B.2s, when it reverted back to the bomber role, in July 1957. Collecting its new aircraft from Coningsby, No 6 returned to Akrotiri, Cyprus as part of the Middle East Air Force. WK109 was finished in the standard overall High Speed Silver scheme, with standard roundels above the wings and on the fuselage sides. The underwing and rear fuselage serial number were both in black. with the 'last three' repeated on the nosewheel doors. Note the No 6 Squadron 'gunner's stripe' across the fin and the red 'flying can-opener' on the wing tip tanks.
Inset: Enlargement of the No 6 Sqn 'flying can-opener' marking on the wing tip tanks.
References used: p74, 'English Electric Canberra' by Ken Delve, Peter Green and John Clemons, Midland Counties Publications, 1992; and p12, 'Bomber Squadrons of the RAF' by Philip J R Moyes, MacDonald & Co Ltd, 1964 (Third impression 1971)

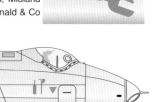

English Electric Canberra T.11, WJ610, of No 228 OCU, RAF Leeming, 1959
Originally manufactured by Handley Page in September 1953, WJ610 was one of eight Canberra B.2s converted into the Airborne Interception trainer version, T.11, and re-issued to 228 OCU. With its distinctive, pointed black fibre glass nose housing the AI radar, WJ610 was otherwise finished in the standard overall High Speed Silver scheme, with 36 inch wide 'Trainer Bands' around the wings and rear fuselage. Standard roundels were carried above the wings and on the fuselage sides and the underwing and rear fuselage serial number were both black. No unit markings were carried other than a black code letter 'G' on the forward fuselage side.

References used: p131, 'English Electric Canberra' by Ken Delve, Peter Green and John Clemons, Midland Counties Publications, 1992

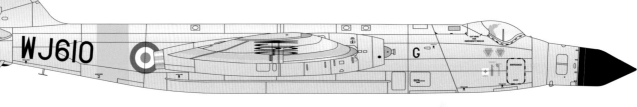

English Electric Canberra PR.3, WE136, of 'C' (PR) Squadron, No 231 OCU, RAF Bassingbourn, January 1958
No 231 OCU was a large unit made up of three squadrons. 'A' and 'B' Squadrons were the 'bomber' Operational Training Units and 'C' Squadron covered the 'photo reconnaissance element'. WE136, which had previously served on No 540 Sqn, was finished in the High Altitude Photo Reconnaissance Scheme of Medium Sea Grey upper surfaces with PRU Blue undersides. Standard roundels were carried above the wings and on the fuselage sides. The underwing and fuselage serial numbers were both in white. Note the 231 OCU 'Cheetah's Head' unit marking on the fin.

Inset: The 231 OCU 'Cheetah's Head' unit marking.

References used: p28, 'English Electric Canberra' by Ken Delve, Peter Green and John Clemons, Midland Counties Publications, 1992

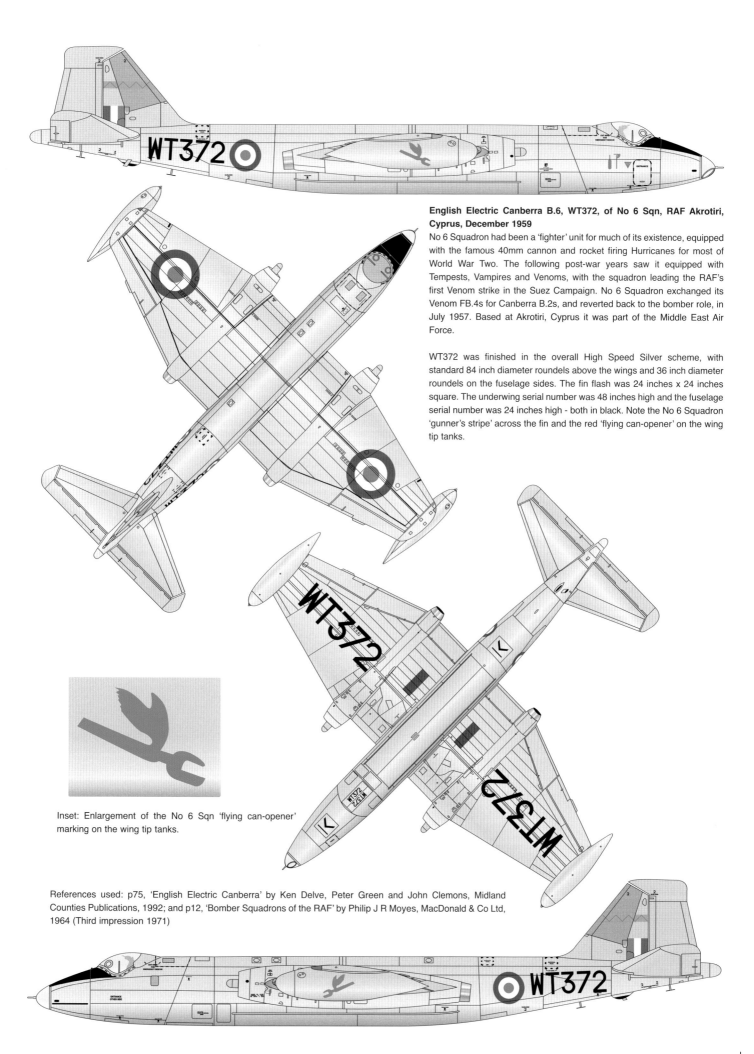

English Electric Canberra B.6, WT372, of No 6 Sqn, RAF Akrotiri, Cyprus, December 1959

No 6 Squadron had been a 'fighter' unit for much of its existence, equipped with the famous 40mm cannon and rocket firing Hurricanes for most of World War Two. The following post-war years saw it equipped with Tempests, Vampires and Venoms, with the squadron leading the RAF's first Venom strike in the Suez Campaign. No 6 Squadron exchanged its Venom FB.4s for Canberra B.2s, and reverted back to the bomber role, in July 1957. Based at Akrotiri, Cyprus it was part of the Middle East Air Force.

WT372 was finished in the overall High Speed Silver scheme, with standard 84 inch diameter roundels above the wings and 36 inch diameter roundels on the fuselage sides. The fin flash was 24 inches x 24 inches square. The underwing serial number was 48 inches high and the fuselage serial number was 24 inches high - both in black. Note the No 6 Squadron 'gunner's stripe' across the fin and the red 'flying can-opener' on the wing tip tanks.

Inset: Enlargement of the No 6 Sqn 'flying can-opener' marking on the wing tip tanks.

References used: p75, 'English Electric Canberra' by Ken Delve, Peter Green and John Clemons, Midland Counties Publications, 1992; and p12, 'Bomber Squadrons of the RAF' by Philip J R Moyes, MacDonald & Co Ltd, 1964 (Third impression 1971)

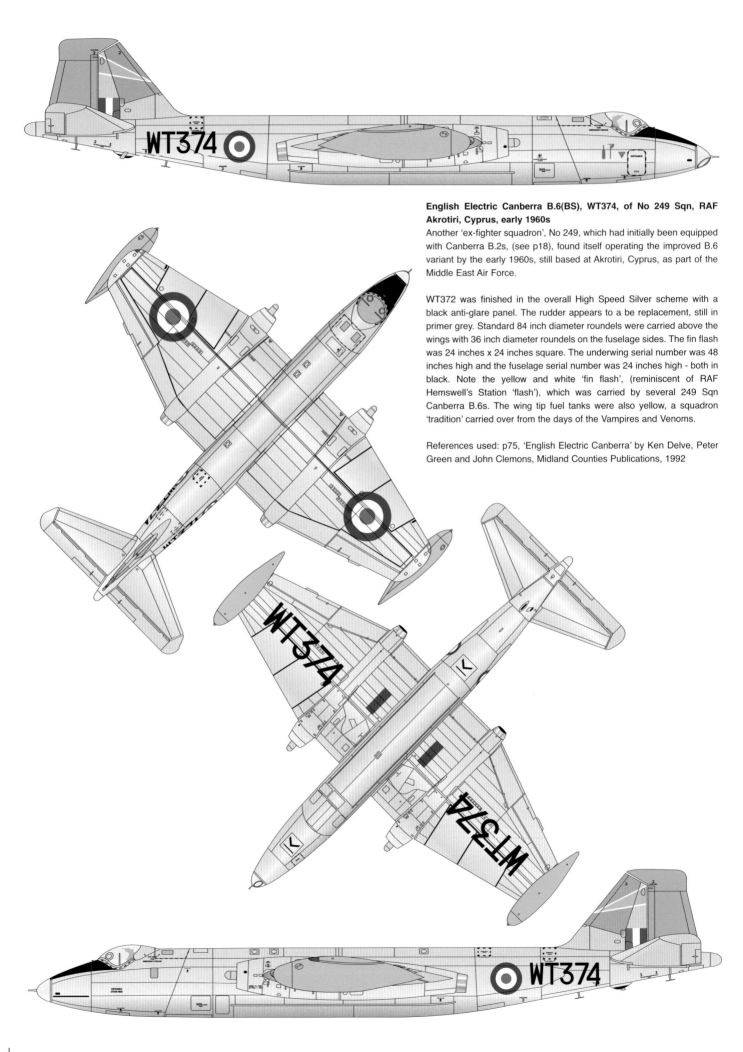

English Electric Canberra B.6(BS), WT374, of No 249 Sqn, RAF Akrotiri, Cyprus, early 1960s

Another 'ex-fighter squadron', No 249, which had initially been equipped with Canberra B.2s, (see p18), found itself operating the improved B.6 variant by the early 1960s, still based at Akrotiri, Cyprus, as part of the Middle East Air Force.

WT372 was finished in the overall High Speed Silver scheme with a black anti-glare panel. The rudder appears to a be replacement, still in primer grey. Standard 84 inch diameter roundels were carried above the wings with 36 inch diameter roundels on the fuselage sides. The fin flash was 24 inches x 24 inches square. The underwing serial number was 48 inches high and the fuselage serial number was 24 inches high - both in black. Note the yellow and white 'fin flash', (reminiscent of RAF Hemswell's Station 'flash'), which was carried by several 249 Sqn Canberra B.6s. The wing tip fuel tanks were also yellow, a squadron 'tradition' carried over from the days of the Vampires and Venoms.

References used: p75, 'English Electric Canberra' by Ken Delve, Peter Green and John Clemons, Midland Counties Publications, 1992

Canberra B.2, XA536, was originally built as a replacement for WD991, which crashed before delivery. It was photographed in the summer of 1970, after conversion to T.19 standard in the markings of No 85 Squadron - see p14.
(Photo: Glenn Sands)

Canberra T.4, WJ870, in the markings of 231 OCU, photographed whilst on loan to that unit in the late 1970s.
(Photo: Glenn Sands)

Canberra B.2, WK130, in the markings of No 35 Squadron, RAF Marham, circa 1955 - see p10.
(Photo: via Glenn Sands)

Canberra B.2, WJ713, finished in overall Aluminium with fluorescent Day-Glo orange 'trainer stripes', photographed whilst serving with No 360 squadron.
(Photo: via Glenn Sands)

Canberra PR.3, WH776 served with the Royal Aircraft Establishment and Royal Radar Establishment before being scrapped in 1972. Note the 'bulge' infront of the fuselage roundel.
(Photo: via Glenn Sands)

Top: WH964, originally built as a Canberra B.6, was progressively modified to B.15 and then upto E.15 standard, as seen here in the markings of No 98 Squadron, No 90 (Signals) Group, in the early 1970s. Also see illustrations on pp36 and 41.
(Photo: via Glenn Sands)

Above Left: Another photo of Canberra B.2, XA536, (see photo at top of p 23), photographed later in her career, resplendent in the fluorescent Day-Glo orange 'trainer stripes'.
(Photo: via Glenn Sands)

Above Right: Canberra PR.7, WJ815 in the markings No 360 Squadron, photographed in July 1978.
(Photo: Glenn Sands)

Left: Canberra T.4, WJ861/Z of No 85 Squadron, photographed in the early 1970s.
(Photo: via Glenn Sands)

Top: Canberra B.15, WJ762, was originally built as a Canberra B.6, and is seen here in the markings of No 73 Squadron whilst serving with the Akrotiri Wing in the early 1960s.
(Photo: via Glenn Sands)

Above Left: Canberra T.4, WJ876, in the striking RAF Trainer Scheme with low-viz Red/Blue national markings, photographed at St Mawgan in the early 1970s.
(Photo: via Glenn Sands)

Above Right: Canberra B.2, WJ762, converted to TT.18 standard, in target towing markings whilst serving with No 7 Squadron in August 1974. Note the Rushton target drone and winch pod under the wing.
(Photo: via Glenn Sands)

Right: WH876 was a converted Canberra T.4, which had served with the Royal Navy as a U.14 and the A&AEE as a U.10 before being photographed in June 1980 whilst acting as a test aircraft with Martin Baker.
(Photo: via Glenn Sands)

Top Left: Canberra B.2, WK162, of No 98 Squadron, No 90 (Signals) Group, RAF Tangmere, circa 1963 - see p36. (Photo: via Glenn Sands)

Top Right: After serving with No 98 Squadron, WK162, was transferred to No 85 Squadron, in whose markings it is seen here. (Photo: via Glenn Sands)

Middle Left: Canberra B.2, WJ678, in the markings of No 100 Squadron in the spring of 1976. (Photo: via Glenn Sands)

Middle Right: Another shot of Canberra B.2, WJ678, now coded C·F, after being repainted in the Dark Green/Dark Sea Grey camouflage scheme with low-viz Red/Blue national markings, circa 1985. (Photo: via Glenn Sands)

Lower Left & Right: Port and starboard views of Canberra TT.18, WJ636, coded C·X, in the markings of No 100 Squadron, whilst based at RAF Marham in the summer of 1990 - see p48. (Photo: via Glenn Sands)

Left: Canberra B.2, WK128, in the 'Raspberry Ripple' upper surfaces and black/yellow target tug under surfaces scheme whilst operating with the Royal Aircraft Establishment at Llanbedr in the spring of 1990. Note the Rushton target drone pods under the wings - see p45. (Photo: via Glenn Sands)

Above: Canberra TT.18, WH887, coded '847', of the Fleet Requirements and Air Direction Unit, RNAS Yeovilton, circa 1985. Note the Rushton target drone pods under the wings - see p47. (Photo: via Glenn Sands)

Right: Canberra B.6, WT309, in an overall white with red nose, rear fuselage and wing tips scheme, photographed whilst probably serving with the A&AEE at Boscombe Down, prior to being sold back to BAC in late 1969 . (Photo: via Glenn Sands)

Below: Canberra TT.18, WK118, of No 100 Squadron, this time in the Dark Green/Dark Sea Grey upper surfaces with black/yellow diagonal striped under surfaces scheme. Note the Rushton target drone pods under the wings - see colour scheme variations on pp42, 44, 45 and 48. (Photo: via Glenn Sands)

Above Right: Canberra TT.18, WK142, of the Fleet Requirements and Air Direction Unit, based at RNAS Yeovilton, circa 1985, but this time in the overall Light Aircraft Grey and Day-Glo orange fluorescent stripes scheme. (Photo: via Glenn Sands)

Right: A long serving Canberra B.2, WH876, finished in another overall white scheme, this time with just a red fuselage cheatline, photographed whilst serving with the Bomber & Maritime Flight Test Squadron, in the summer of 1967. (Photo: via Glenn Sands)

Above and below: Two long-nosed Canberra conversions used by RAE Bedford. Above WT333, originally started life as a B(I)8, but was modified to long-nosed B.6 configuration in 1976, whilst Canberra B.2, (below) WH953 was fitted with an AI Mk 20 radar nose in 1984. (Photos: via Glenn Sands)

Below and back cover: Canberra T.17, WD955, 'EM' of No 360 Squadron in the Camouflage Beige (Hemp) and Light Aircraft Grey scheme based at RAF Wyton in late 1991. (Photos via Denis Calvert).

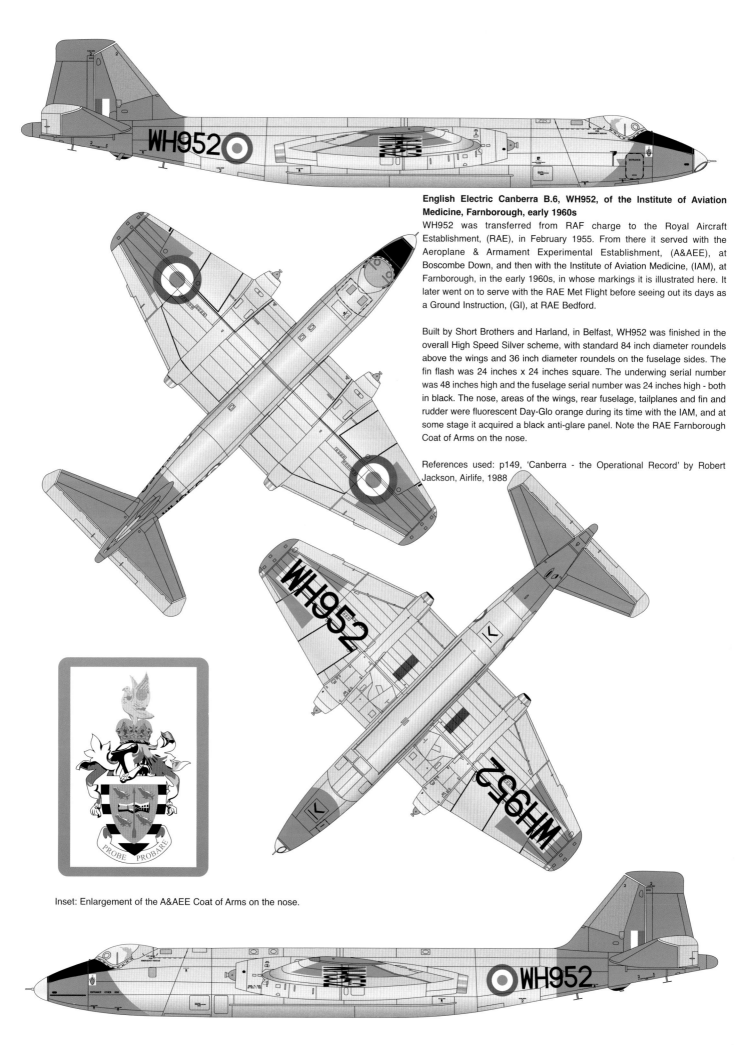

English Electric Canberra B.6, WH952, of the Institute of Aviation Medicine, Farnborough, early 1960s

WH952 was transferred from RAF charge to the Royal Aircraft Establishment, (RAE), in February 1955. From there it served with the Aeroplane & Armament Experimental Establishment, (A&AEE), at Boscombe Down, and then with the Institute of Aviation Medicine, (IAM), at Farnborough, in the early 1960s, in whose markings it is illustrated here. It later went on to serve with the RAE Met Flight before seeing out its days as a Ground Instruction, (GI), at RAE Bedford.

Built by Short Brothers and Harland, in Belfast, WH952 was finished in the overall High Speed Silver scheme, with standard 84 inch diameter roundels above the wings and 36 inch diameter roundels on the fuselage sides. The fin flash was 24 inches x 24 inches square. The underwing serial number was 48 inches high and the fuselage serial number was 24 inches high - both in black. The nose, areas of the wings, rear fuselage, tailplanes and fin and rudder were fluorescent Day-Glo orange during its time with the IAM, and at some stage it acquired a black anti-glare panel. Note the RAE Farnborough Coat of Arms on the nose.

References used: p149, 'Canberra - the Operational Record' by Robert Jackson, Airlife, 1988

Inset: Enlargement of the A&AEE Coat of Arms on the nose.

English Electric Canberra T.4, WH706, of No 45 Sqn, RAF Tengah, Singapore, early 1960s
Most Canberra bomber squadrons had one or two dual control variants for 'on squadron' refresher training. Originally built as a B.2 in 1953, WH706 was modified in to a T.4 in 1956 and was
posted to No 45 Sqn, Far East Air Force, based at Tengah, Singapore. Almost uniquely, it was finished in an overall white scheme with a black anti-glare panel, and 8 inch wide fluorescent 'Day-Glo' stripes on the nose, rear fuselage, fin and possibly the wing leading edges. Standard roundels were carried above the wings on the fuselage sides. The underwing and fuselage serial number were both in black. Note the 45 Sqn winged Camel and 'Camel Air' legend on the forward fuselage.

References used: p99, 'English Electric Canberra' by Ken Delve, Peter Green and John Clemons, Midland Counties Publications, 1992

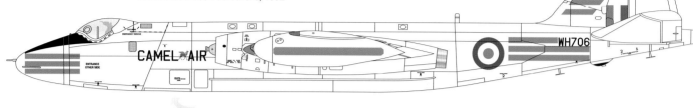

English Electric Canberra B(I)6, WT319, of No 213 Sqn, RAF(G) Ahlhorn, Germany, August 1957
No 213 was re-formed as a 2 TAF bomber/intruder squadron, receiving its first Canberra B(I)6s in March 1956. WT319 was finished in the overall High Speed Silver scheme with standard roundels above the wings and on the fuselage sides. The underwing and fuselage serial numbers were both in black. Note the black painted four 20mm Hispano cannon gun pack fitted over the rear bomb bay and lack of wing tip fuel tanks.
References used: p252, 'English Electric Canberra' by Ken Delve, Peter Green and John Clemons, Midland Counties Publications, 1992

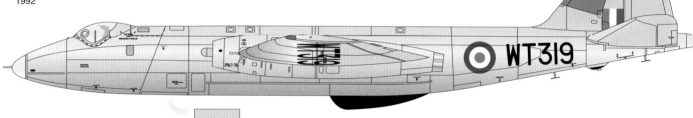

English Electric Canberra B.2, WJ640, of No 51 (Special Duties) Squadron, Royal Air Force Signals Command, (RAFSC), RAF Watton, early 1960s
When No 192 Squadron was re-numbered as No 51 Sqn in August 1958, it also took on a new role as a 'Special Duties' radar reconnaissance unit, equipped with Avro Lincoln B.2s, and both the Canberra B.2 and B.6 variants. Canberra B.2, WJ640, on strength during the early 1960s, was finished in the overall High Speed Silver scheme with a black anti-glare panel. Standard roundels were carried above the wings and on the fuselage sides. The underwing and fuselage serial numbers were both in black - in a 'squared-off' style. Note the 'Royal Air Force Signals Command' legend on the fuselage sides, in black, and the No 51 Sqn, red 'Flying Goose', emblem on the fin.
Inset: Enlargement of the No 51 Sqn, red 'Flying Goose', emblem on the fin.
References used: p50, 'English Electric Canberra' by Ken Delve, Peter Green and John Clemons, Midland Counties Publications, 1992

English Electric Canberra B.2, WD988, of No 73 Sqn, RAF Akrotiri, Cyprus, September 1958
Illustrated as she looked when photographed at El Adem, in September 1958, WD988 was then finished in an experimental overall gloss white scheme, a feature which led to it being dubbed 'Moby Dick' within the squadron! Standard roundels were carried above the wings on the fuselage sides. Although the underwing serial number may have remained in black, it is thought that the fuselage serial number was in 'roundel' blue. Note the No 73 Sqn 'talbot', (an heraldic dog), in a shield on the fin, and the two-tone blue spearhead marking on the wing tip tank.

Inset: Enlargement of the No 73 Sqn 'talbot', (heraldic dog), in a shield on the fin.
References used: p74, 'English Electric Canberra' by Ken Delve, Peter Green and John Clemons, Midland Counties Publications, 1992; and p101, 'Bomber Squadrons of the RAF' by Philip J R Moyes, MacDonald & Co Ltd, 1964 (Third impression 1971)

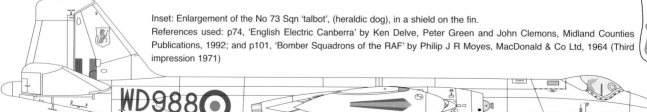

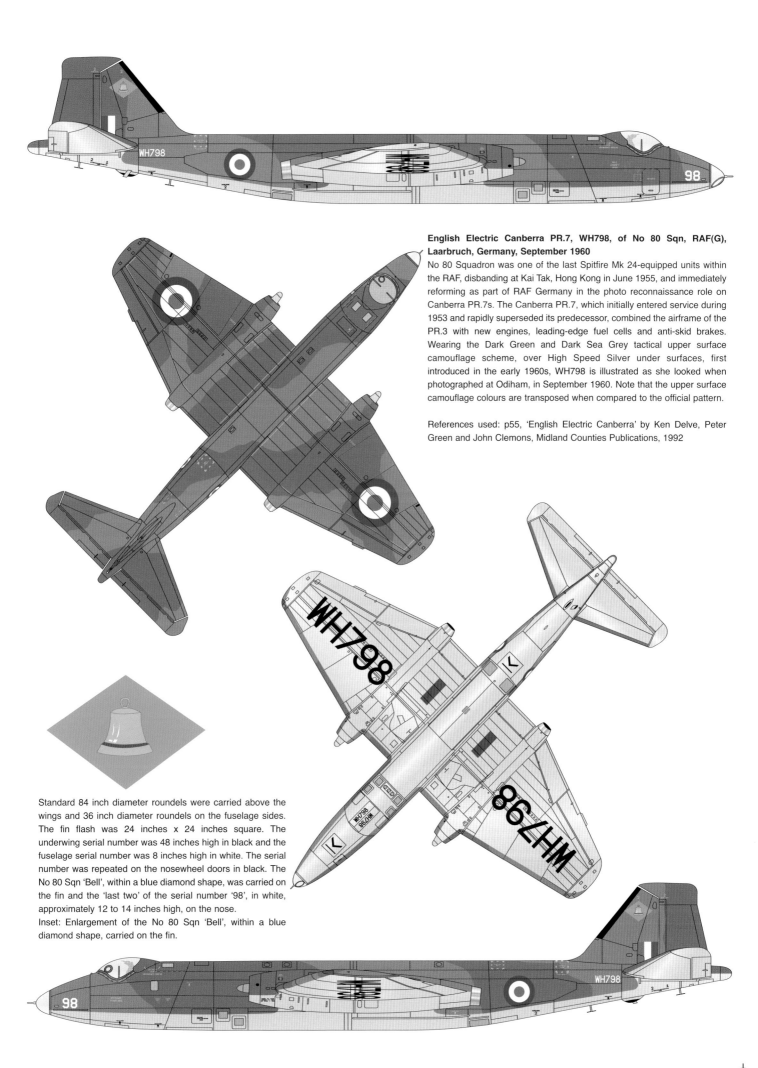

English Electric Canberra PR.7, WH798, of No 80 Sqn, RAF(G), Laarbruch, Germany, September 1960

No 80 Squadron was one of the last Spitfire Mk 24-equipped units within the RAF, disbanding at Kai Tak, Hong Kong in June 1955, and immediately reforming as part of RAF Germany in the photo reconnaissance role on Canberra PR.7s. The Canberra PR.7, which initially entered service during 1953 and rapidly superseded its predecessor, combined the airframe of the PR.3 with new engines, leading-edge fuel cells and anti-skid brakes. Wearing the Dark Green and Dark Sea Grey tactical upper surface camouflage scheme, over High Speed Silver under surfaces, first introduced in the early 1960s, WH798 is illustrated as she looked when photographed at Odiham, in September 1960. Note that the upper surface camouflage colours are transposed when compared to the official pattern.

References used: p55, 'English Electric Canberra' by Ken Delve, Peter Green and John Clemons, Midland Counties Publications, 1992

Standard 84 inch diameter roundels were carried above the wings and 36 inch diameter roundels on the fuselage sides. The fin flash was 24 inches x 24 inches square. The underwing serial number was 48 inches high in black and the fuselage serial number was 8 inches high in white. The serial number was repeated on the nosewheel doors in black. The No 80 Sqn 'Bell', within a blue diamond shape, was carried on the fin and the 'last two' of the serial number '98', in white, approximately 12 to 14 inches high, on the nose.
Inset: Enlargement of the No 80 Sqn 'Bell', within a blue diamond shape, carried on the fin.

English Electric Canberra T.4, WT480, of the Central Flying School, (CFS), RAF Thorney Island, May 1960
WT480 was built as a T.4 from the outset, and following brief service with No 102 Sqn, was transferred to the Central Flying School, in whose colours it is illustrated here. Finished in the overall High Speed Silver scheme, with standard roundels above the wings and on the fuselage sides, areas of fluorescent 'Day-Glo' orange were applied to the nose, areas of the wings, rear fuselage, tailplanes and fin and rudder. The underwing and rear fuselage serial number were both in black as were the codes C·C either side of the fuselage roundel.

References used: p126, 'Canberra - the Operational Record' by Robert Jackson, Airlife, 1988

English Electric Canberra B.2, WH670, of No 245 Sqn, Royal Air Force Signals Command, RAF Tangmere, circa 1961
No 245 Sqn was re-formed in August 1958, simply by re-numbering No 527 Sqn, and served as a radar calibration unit until April 1963 when it was itself re-numbered, as No 98 Sqn, (see p34). WH670, which went on to fly some 10,000 hours before being scrapped in October 1991, was finished in the High Altitude Day Bomber Scheme of Medium Sea Grey and Light Slate Grey upper surfaces with PRU Blue undersides. Roundels were carried above the wings and on the fuselage sides, with the serial number, in white, under the wings and on the rear fuselage sides. Other than the 'Royal Air Force Signals Command' legend on the fuselage sides, no other squadron or station markings appear to have been carried.

References used: p137, 'English Electric Canberra' by Ken Delve, Peter Green and John Clemons, Midland Counties Publications, 1992

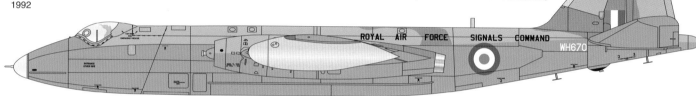

English Electric Canberra U.14, WH921, of No 728B NAS, Fleet Air Arm, Hal Far, Malta, summer 1961
No 728B NAS was one of only two FAA units to operate unmanned 'target' variants of the Canberra. WH921 was converted from a B.2 into U.14 in March 1961and was shot down by a 'Sea Slug' missile fired from *HMS Girdleness*, on 6 October of the same year. WH921 was finished in an overall white scheme with red wing bands. Standard roundels were carried above the wings on the fuselage sides.

References used: p119, 'English Electric Canberra' by Ken Delve, Peter Green and John Clemons, Midland Counties Publications, 1992

English Electric Canberra B.16, WJ774, of No 249 Sqn, RAF Akrotiri, Cyprus, 1962
WJ774 was originally built as B.6(BS), and served with No 249 Sqn before being converted to B.16 standard and returned to the squadron. Wearing the Dark Green and Dark Sea Grey tactical upper surface camouflage scheme, over High Speed Silver under surfaces, WJ774 is illustrated as she looked in September 1962. Standard roundels were carried above the wings and on the fuselage sides. The underwing serials were black and the fuselage serials white. The No 249 Sqn 'Running Elephant', marking was carried on the fin.

Inset: Enlargement of the No 249 Sqn 'Running Elephant', marking on the fin.
References used: p89, 'English Electric Canberra' by Ken Delve, Peter Green and John Clemons, Midland Counties Publications, 1992

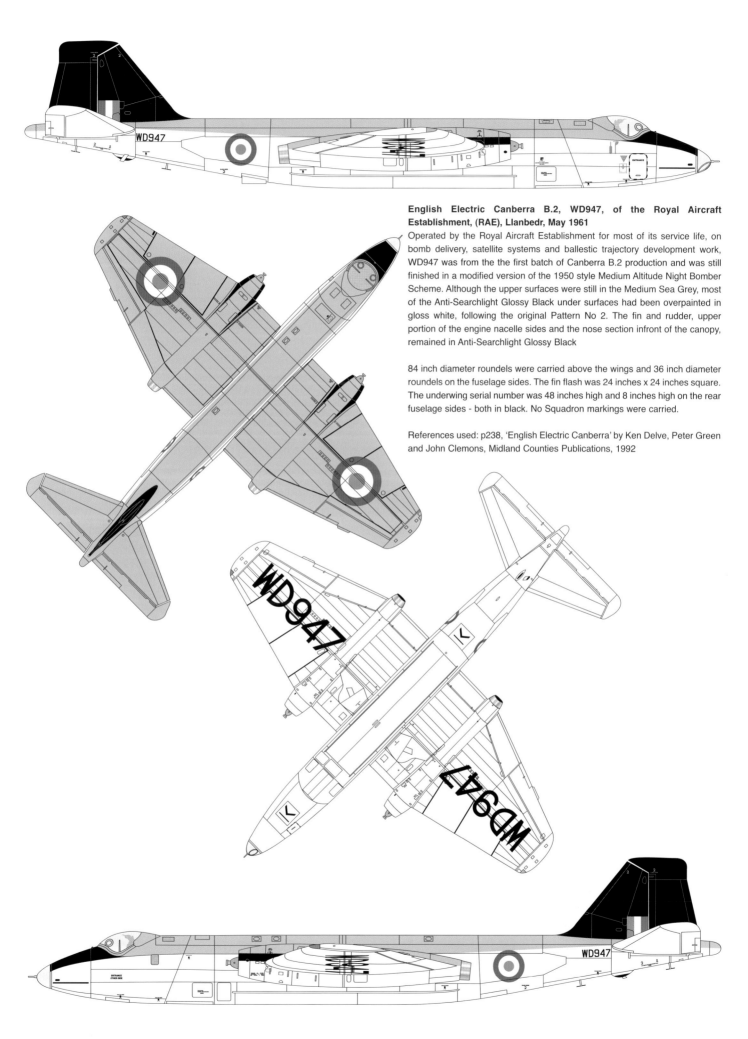

English Electric Canberra B.2, WD947, of the Royal Aircraft Establishment, (RAE), Llanbedr, May 1961

Operated by the Royal Aircraft Establishment for most of its service life, on bomb delivery, satellite systems and ballistic trajectory development work, WD947 was from the the first batch of Canberra B.2 production and was still finished in a modified version of the 1950 style Medium Altitude Night Bomber Scheme. Although the upper surfaces were still in the Medium Sea Grey, most of the Anti-Searchlight Glossy Black under surfaces had been overpainted in gloss white, following the original Pattern No 2. The fin and rudder, upper portion of the engine nacelle sides and the nose section infront of the canopy, remained in Anti-Searchlight Glossy Black

84 inch diameter roundels were carried above the wings and 36 inch diameter roundels on the fuselage sides. The fin flash was 24 inches x 24 inches square. The underwing serial number was 48 inches high and 8 inches high on the rear fuselage sides - both in black. No Squadron markings were carried.

References used: p238, 'English Electric Canberra' by Ken Delve, Peter Green and John Clemons, Midland Counties Publications, 1992

English Electric Canberra B.2, WH727, of the Station Flight, Khormaksar, Aden, circa mid-1960s

As part of the Khormaksar Station Flight, WH727 was regularly used by the AOC Aden, Sir David Lee. It was finished in an experimental overall gloss white scheme, originally applied to try and reduce cockpit temperatures in the hot Middle Eastern sun. Nicknamed 'Queen of the Arabian Skies', it carried standard roundels above the wings and on the fuselage sides. The underwing and fuselage serial number were both in black. Note the black anti-glare panel infront of the cockpit,

References used: p89, 'English Electric Canberra' by Ken Delve, Peter Green and John Clemons, Midland Counties Publications, 1992

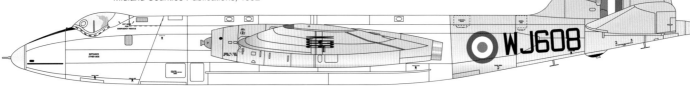

English Electric Canberra B.2, WJ608, of the Swifter Flight, Middle East Air Force, El Adem, Libya, mid-1960s

One of the least known of Canberra activities, was that of the 'Swifter Flight', which operated seven Canberra B.2s on low-level, high speed trials, during the early/mid 1960s. WJ608 is illustrated here as she looked when she was photographed refuelling at El Adem in Libya, finished in the overall High Speed Silver scheme with a gloss white forward fuselage section. Standard roundels were carried above the wings and on the fuselage sides. The underwing and fuselage serial number were both in black. Note the narrow black anti-glare panel infront of the cockpit and the 'Swifter Flight' emblem on the fin.
Inset: Enlargement of the 'Swifter Flight' emblem on the fin.
References used: p127, 'English Electric Canberra' by Ken Delve, Peter Green and John Clemons, Midland Counties Publications, 1992

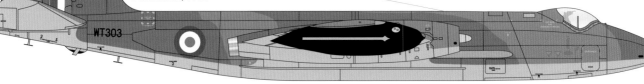

English Electric Canberra B.16, WT303, of No 249 Sqn, RAF Akrotiri, Cyprus, mid-1960s

WT303 was another original B.6(BS) converted up to B.16 standard, and issued to No 249 when the squadron was re-equipped with this upgraded and 'tropicalised' variant. Wearing the Dark Green and Dark Sea Grey tactical upper surface camouflage scheme, over the newly introduced Light Aircraft Grey under surfaces, WT303 is illustrated as she looked circa 1964. Standard roundels were carried above the wings and on the fuselage sides. The underwing and the fuselage serials were black and repeated on the nosewheel doors. Note the strake on the forward fuselage side which was part of the 'Blue Shadow' fit. The No 249 Sqn 'Running Elephant', marking was carried within a yellow disc on the black painted fin and the black wing tip tanks sported a yellow 'spear', (agassi?).
Inset: Enlargement of the No 249 Sqn 'Running Elephant', marking on the fin.
References used: p77, 'English Electric Canberra' by Ken Delve, Peter Green and John Clemons, Midland Counties Publications, 1992

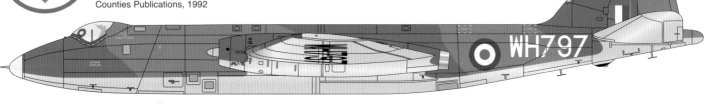

English Electric Canberra PR.7, WH797, of No 81 Sqn, RAF Tengah, Malaya, mid-1960s

No 81 Sqn was part of the Far East Air Force, and was equipped with Canberra PR.7s from January 1960 until January 1970. WH797 is illustrated finished in the Dark Green and Dark Sea Grey tactical upper surface camouflage scheme, (in the correct pattern), over High Speed Silver under surfaces. Standard roundels were carried above the wings and on the fuselage sides. The underwing serials were black and the fuselage serials were white. No 81's 'red star and dagger', marking was carried within a white disc on the fin.

Inset: Enlargement of the No 81 Squadron's 'red star and dagger', marking on the fin.

References used: p101, 'English Electric Canberra' by Ken Delve, Peter Green and John Clemons, Midland Counties Publications, 1992

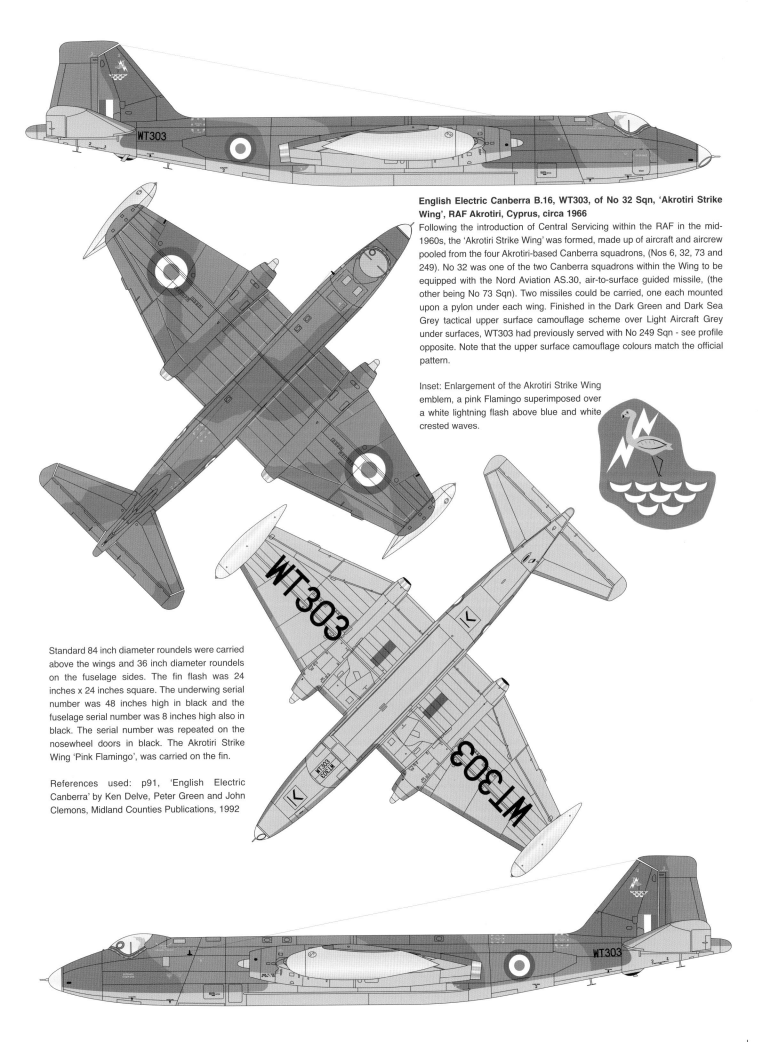

English Electric Canberra B.16, WT303, of No 32 Sqn, 'Akrotiri Strike Wing', RAF Akrotiri, Cyprus, circa 1966

Following the introduction of Central Servicing within the RAF in the mid-1960s, the 'Akrotiri Strike Wing' was formed, made up of aircraft and aircrew pooled from the four Akrotiri-based Canberra squadrons, (Nos 6, 32, 73 and 249). No 32 was one of the two Canberra squadrons within the Wing to be equipped with the Nord Aviation AS.30, air-to-surface guided missile, (the other being No 73 Sqn). Two missiles could be carried, one each mounted upon a pylon under each wing. Finished in the Dark Green and Dark Sea Grey tactical upper surface camouflage scheme over Light Aircraft Grey under surfaces, WT303 had previously served with No 249 Sqn - see profile opposite. Note that the upper surface camouflage colours match the official pattern.

Inset: Enlargement of the Akrotiri Strike Wing emblem, a pink Flamingo superimposed over a white lightning flash above blue and white crested waves.

Standard 84 inch diameter roundels were carried above the wings and 36 inch diameter roundels on the fuselage sides. The fin flash was 24 inches x 24 inches square. The underwing serial number was 48 inches high in black and the fuselage serial number was 8 inches high also in black. The serial number was repeated on the nosewheel doors in black. The Akrotiri Strike Wing 'Pink Flamingo', was carried on the fin.

References used: p91, 'English Electric Canberra' by Ken Delve, Peter Green and John Clemons, Midland Counties Publications, 1992

English Electric Canberra B.2, WK162, of No 98 Sqn, No 90 (Signals) Group, RAF Tangmere, circa 1963

Created by re-numbering No 245 Sqn in April 1963, No 98 Sqn continued to serve in the unglamorous but essential, radar calibration role. WK162 was finished in Dark Green and Dark Sea Grey upper surfaces over Light Aircraft Grey under surfaces, with Day-Glo fluorescent orange stripes on the nose, rear fuselage, fin and wings. Standard roundels were carried above the wings and on the fuselage sides. The underwing and the fuselage serial number were both in black. The No 98 Sqn 'Cerberus', marking was carried on the nose, flanked by white 'zig-zags' on a red bar.

Inset: Enlargement of the 'Cerberus', marking flanked by white 'zig-zags' on a red bar, on the nose.

References used: p139, 'English Electric Canberra' by Ken Delve, Peter Green and John Clemons, Midland Counties Publications, 1992

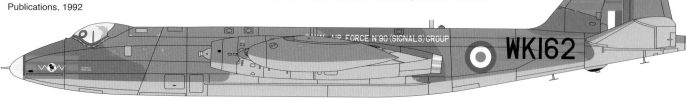

English Electric Canberra T.11, WH904, of No 85 Sqn, RAF Binbrook, September 1965

Operating a mix of Meteors and Canberras, No 85 Sqn re-formed as a Target Facilities unit in April 1963, acting as 'targets' for radar controllers and during exercises. WH904 was originally built as a B.2, converted to T.11 standard, (as illustrated here), and converted yet again to T.19 standard. It is currently on display at Newark Air Museum. Finished in the overall High Speed Silver scheme, WH904 carried standard roundels above and below the wings and on the fuselage sides. The underwing and fuselage serial numbers were both in black, and repeated on the nosewheel doors. No 85 Squadron's red and black checks were applied either side of the fuselage roundel with the Squadron badge on the forward fuselage.

Inset: Enlargement of the No 85 Sqn badge on the forward fuselage.

References used: p131, 'English Electric Canberra' by Ken Delve, Peter Green and John Clemons, Midland Counties Publications, 1992

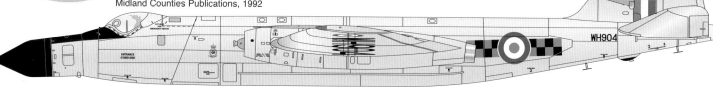

English Electric Canberra PR.7, WH801, of No 31 Sqn, RAF(G) Laarbruch, Germany, mid-1960s

No 31 Squadron operated the Canberra PR.7 in the low-level photo recce role, for over fifteen years, from March 1955 until it disbanded as a PR unit in March 1971. WH801 is illustrated finished in the Dark Green and Dark Sea Grey tactical upper surface camouflage scheme over High Speed Silver under surfaces. Standard roundels were carried above the wings and on the fuselage sides. The underwing serials were black and the fuselage serials were white. No 31's yellow 'star' marking was carried within a black disc on the fin.

Inset: Enlargement of the No 31 Squadron's yellow 'star', marking on the fin.

References used: Title page, 'English Electric Canberra' by Ken Delve, Peter Green and John Clemons, Midland Counties Publications, 1992

English Electric Canberra PR.7, WT534, of No 17 Sqn, RAF(G) Wildenrath, Germany, mid-1960s

No 17 Squadron re-formed at Whan in Germany as a photo reconnaissance unit in June 1956, equipped with Canberra PR.7s, but moved to Wildenrath in April of the following year, where it stayed, as part of 2 TAF, still operating the PR.7, until it disbanded in June 1969. Finished in Dark Green and Dark Sea Grey upper surfaces over High Speed Silver under surfaces, standard roundels were carried above the wings and on the fuselage sides. The underwing serials were black and the fuselage serials were white. No 17 Sqn's red 'gauntlet' marking flanked by black wavy lines, was carried within a white disc, on the fin.

Inset: Enlargement of the No 17 Squadron's red 'gauntlet' marking on the fin.

References used: p55, 'English Electric Canberra' by Ken Delve, Peter Green and John Clemons, Midland Counties Publications, 1992

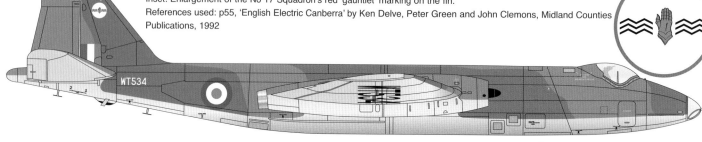

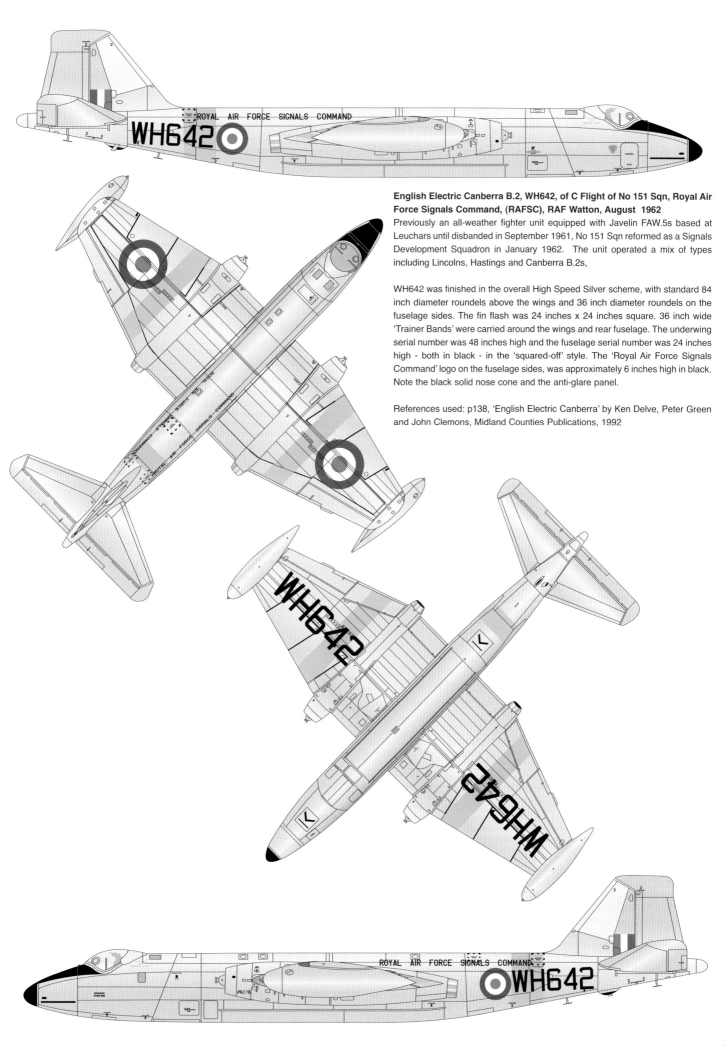

English Electric Canberra B.2, WH642, of C Flight of No 151 Sqn, Royal Air Force Signals Command, (RAFSC), RAF Watton, August 1962

Previously an all-weather fighter unit equipped with Javelin FAW.5s based at Leuchars until disbanded in September 1961, No 151 Sqn reformed as a Signals Development Squadron in January 1962. The unit operated a mix of types including Lincolns, Hastings and Canberra B.2s,

WH642 was finished in the overall High Speed Silver scheme, with standard 84 inch diameter roundels above the wings and 36 inch diameter roundels on the fuselage sides. The fin flash was 24 inches x 24 inches square. 36 inch wide 'Trainer Bands' were carried around the wings and rear fuselage. The underwing serial number was 48 inches high and the fuselage serial number was 24 inches high - both in black - in the 'squared-off' style. The 'Royal Air Force Signals Command' logo on the fuselage sides, was approximately 6 inches high in black. Note the black solid nose cone and the anti-glare panel.

References used: p138, 'English Electric Canberra' by Ken Delve, Peter Green and John Clemons, Midland Counties Publications, 1992

English Electric Canberra B.15, XK641, of No 45 Sqn, RAF Tengah, Singapore, early 1966

Illustrated as she looked when photographed on one of the squadron's regular detatchments to Labuan, an island off Brunei, XK641, was a one-off B.6 built by English Electric in 1955 and subsequently upgraded to B.15 standard. Finished in Dark Green and Dark Sea Grey upper surfaces over High Speed Silver under surfaces, standard roundels were carried above the wings and on the fuselage sides. The underwing and fuselage serials were black. No 45 Sqn's aircraft were regularly armed with Matra SNEB 68mm rocket pods on the wing pylons during this period. Note the 'last three' of the serial number on the nosewheel doors.

Inset: No 45 Squadron's 'Winged Camel' carried on the fin.

References used: p105, 'English Electric Canberra' by Ken Delve, Peter Green and John Clemons, Midland Counties Publications, 1992

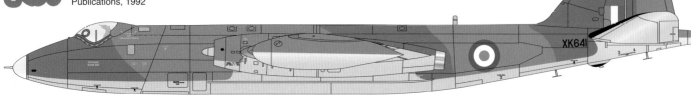

64I

English Electric Canberra PR.7, WH794, of No 58 Sqn, RAF Wyton, late 1966

WH749 was amongst the first Canberra PR.7s to be finished in Dark Green and Dark Sea Grey upper surfaces over Light Aircraft Grey under surfaces from the previous overall High Speed Silver scheme. Standard roundels were carried above the wings and on the fuselage sides. The underwing and fuselage serials were black. The serial number was repeated on the nosewheel doors. No 58 Sqn's 'Owl' marking was carried within a white disc on the fin. Note the red engine intake 'bullets' and the white shield on the nose whose details are unfortunately undiscernable on the reference photograph.

Inset: Enlargement of No 58 Squadron's 'Owl' marking on the fin.

References used: p112, 'English Electric Canberra' by Ken Delve, Peter Green and John Clemons, Midland Counties Publications, 1992

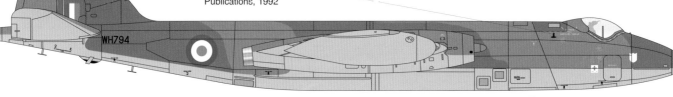

WH794

English Electric Canberra B.6(Mod), WH945, of No 97 Squadron, Royal Air Force Signals Command, (RAFSC), RAF Watton, 1966

Continuing with its 'Special Duties' role, No 97 Sqn received Canberra B.6, WH945, which had been specially modified with a 56 inch nose extension, housing the 'Blue Silk' ASV Mk 21 anti-submarine radar. Finished in the overall High Speed Silver scheme with a black anti-glare panel, it carried Day-Glo fluorescent orange stripes on the nose, rear fuselage, fin and wings. Standard roundels were carried above the wings and on the fuselage sides. The underwing and fuselage serial numbers were both in black. Note the 'Royal Air Force Signals Command' legend on the fuselage sides, in black.

References used: p138, 'English Electric Canberra' by Ken Delve, Peter Green and John Clemons, Midland Counties Publications, 1992

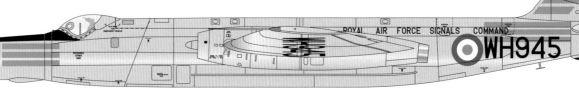

English Electric Canberra PR.7, WT533, of No 17 Sqn, RAF(G), Wildenrath, Germany, 1967

Presumably a participant in the 1967 'Sassoon Photographic Reconnaissance Trophy' competition, WT533 was finished in Dark Green and Dark Sea Grey upper surfaces over High Speed Silver under surfaces. Standard roundels were carried above the wings and on the fuselage sides. The underwing serials were black and fuselage serials white. The 'last three' of the serial number was repeated on the nosewheel doors. No 17 Sqn's 'red gauntlet' marking was carried within a white disc on the fin and repeated on the nose, flanked by black 'zig-zag' lines on white bars. Note the 'Sassoon 67' legend in white on the nose.

Inset: Enlargement of No 17 Squadron's 'red gauntlet' marking on the nose.

References used: p268, 'English Electric Canberra' by Ken Delve, Peter Green and John Clemons, Midland Counties Publications, 1992

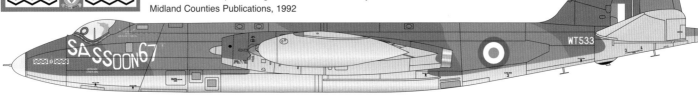

533

English Electric Canberra B.15, WH966, of the Akrotiri Strike Wing, RAF Akrotiri, Cyprus, 1967
WH966 was nominally on No 32 Squadron's charge, and had been modified up to B.15 standard before serving with the Near East Air Force, on Cyprus. It was finished in Dark Green and Dark Sea Grey upper surfaces over High Speed Silver under surfaces. Standard roundels were carried above the wings and on the fuselage sides. The underwing and fuselage serials were black, and repeated on the nosewheel doors. The Akrotiri Strike Wing 'Pink Flamingo' was carried on the fin. Note the 'silver patch' over the fin flash.

Inset: Enlargement of the Akrotiri Strike Wing emblem, a pink Flamingo superimposed over a white lightning flash above blue and white crested waves.
References used: p88, 'English Electric Canberra' by Ken Delve, Peter Green and John Clemons, Midland Counties Publications, 1992

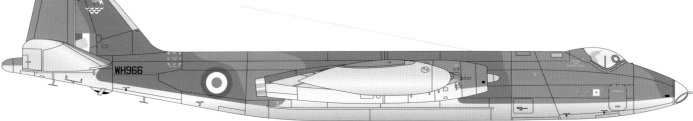

English Electric Canberra B.15, WH948, of the Akrotiri Strike Wing, RAF Akrotiri, Cyprus, September 1967
An 'ex'-32, 249 and 73 Squadron machine, modified up to B.15 standard before serving with the Near East Air Force on Cyprus, WH948 went on to serve with Nos 45, 98 and 100 squadrons, before crashing near Coltishall in August 1988. Finished in Dark Green and Dark Sea Grey upper surfaces over High Speed Silver under surfaces, it carried standard roundels above the wings and on the fuselage sides. The underwing and fuselage serials were black. The Akrotiri Strike Wing 'Pink Flamingo' was carried on the fin. Note the red engine intake 'bullets'.
Inset: Enlargement of the Akrotiri Strike Wing emblem, a pink Flamingo superimposed over a white lightning flash above blue and white crested waves.
References used: p200, 'English Electric Canberra' by Ken Delve, Peter Green and John Clemons, Midland Counties Publications, 1992

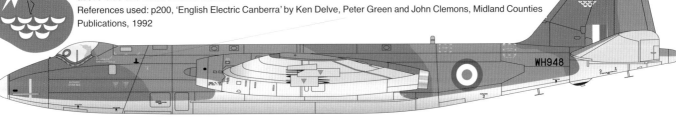

English Electric Canberra B.2, WH715, of the Empire Test Pilots School, (ETPS), Royal Aircraft Establishment, Farnborough, 1967
WH715 spent much of its life as a research and development airframe with the RAE and A&AEE before serving with the Empire Test Pilots School, first at Farnborough and then at Boscombe Down. Finished in the overall High Speed Silver scheme, with standard roundels above the wings and on the fuselage sides, the underwing and the fuselage serial number were in black. Note the 'Empire Test Pilots School' legend on the nose and the numeral '27', both in black .

References used: p242, 'English Electric Canberra' by Ken Delve, Peter Green and John Clemons, Midland Counties Publications, 1992

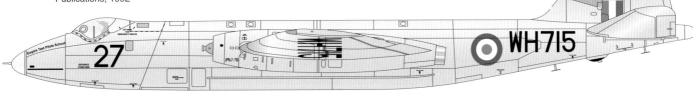

English Electric Canberra B.16, XH570, of the Akrotiri Strike Wing, RAF Akrotiri, Cyprus, 1968
One of a small batch of four B.6s built by English Electric, XH570 was converted up to B.16 standard and was nominally on No 249 Sqn's charge whilst serving with the Akrotiri Strike Wing, despite displaying a stylised version of No 6 Sqn's 'flying can-opener' on the fin when it was photographed in 1968! Finished in Dark Green and Dark Sea Grey upper surfaces over High Speed Silver under surfaces, it carried standard roundels above the wings and on the fuselage sides. The underwing and fuselage serials were black, and were repeated on the nosewheel doors.
Inset: Enlargement of the stylised No 6 Squadron 'flying can-opener' emblem, carried on the fin.
References used: p79, 'English Electric Canberra' by Ken Delve, Peter Green and John Clemons, Midland Counties Publications, 1992

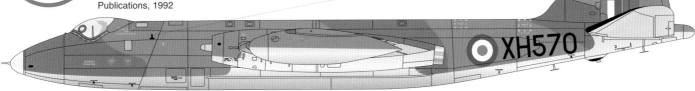

English Electric Canberra B.15, WH971, of the Akrotiri Strike Wing, RAF Akrotiri, Cyprus, April 1968

Another 'anonymous' Akrotiri Strike Wing machine, this time nominally on No 32 Squadron's 'books', WH971 bounced on landing, swung off the runway and crashed, Cat 5, on 24 April 1968. The crew were unhurt. Dark Green and Dark Sea Grey upper surfaces over Light Aircraft Grey under surfaces, it still had High Speed Silver wing tip tanks. Standard roundels were carried above the wings and on the fuselage sides. The underwing and fuselage serials were black. The Akrotiri Strike Wing 'Pink Flamingo' was carried on the fin.

Inset: Enlargement of the Akrotiri Strike Wing emblem, a pink Flamingo superimposed over a white lightning flash above blue and white crested waves.

References used: p80, 'English Electric Canberra' by Ken Delve, Peter Green and John Clemons, Midland Counties Publications, 1992

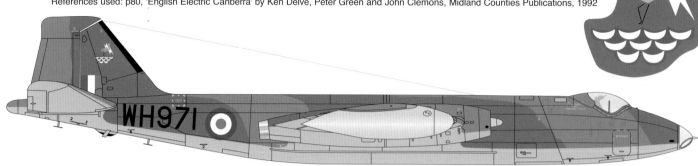

English Electric Canberra T.19, WH714, of No 85 Squadron, RAF Binbrook, June 1968

In its role as a Target Facilities unit, No 85 Squadron continued to use various sub-types of Canberras throughout the late 1960s in this unglamorous, but essential, part of RAF training. At least the colour scheme was striking, comprising High Speed Silver upper surfaces with yellow 'Trainer Bands' around the wings and rear fuselage. The under surfaces were also yellow with broad black diagonal stripes. Standard roundels were carried above the wings and on the fuselage sides. The underwing and the fuselage serial number were in black. Note the black anti-glare panel and the Rushton target-towing winch and 'target' on the port pylon.

References used: p131, 'English Electric Canberra' by Ken Delve, Peter Green and John Clemons, Midland Counties Publications, 1992

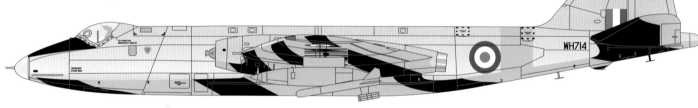

English Electric Canberra B.2, 7913M, (previously WK132), of No 1 School of Technical Training, (SoTT), RAF Halton, 1968

Several retired Canberra airframes were relegated to ground instructional training purposes and given an 'M' suffix serial. This particular B.2, previously serialled WK132, had served with Nos 61 and 15 Squadrons before becoming '7913M' in June 1966 and assigned to No 1 SoTT. It retained its original overall High Speed Silver finish with standard roundels above the wings and on the fuselage sides. The underwing and fuselage 'M' suffix serial number was in black. Note the 'Honington Pheasant' on the fin and the No 1 SoTT numeral '6' on the nose.

References used: p258, 'English Electric Canberra' by Ken Delve, Peter Green and John Clemons, Midland Counties Publications, 1992

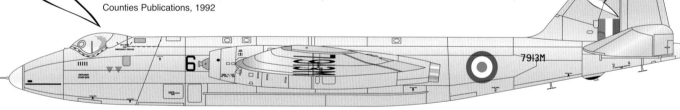

English Electric Canberra B.6, WH952, of the Royal Aircraft Establishment, (RAE), Bedford, circa 1969

Another Canberra that saw very little RAF service as such, spending most of its life as a test-bed for various procedures such as fatigue investigation, wing pylon installation and bomb bay door buffeting with various civil and experimental establishments. WH952 was finished in the overall High Speed Silver scheme with a 'Day-Glo' orange nose area. Standard roundels were carried above the wings and on the fuselage sides. The underwing and rear fuselage serial number were both in black.

References used: p245, 'English Electric Canberra' by Ken Delve, Peter Green and John Clemons, Midland Counties Publications, 1992

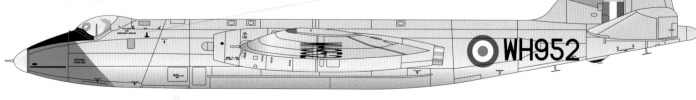

English Electric Canberra B.16, WJ777, of the Akrotiri Strike Wing, RAF Akrotiri, Cyprus, January 1969

The Akrotiri Strike Wing was disbanded at the end of February 1969 and WJ777 was selected for the 10 January disbandment parade flypast. To commemorate the event, the aircraft displayed the badges of the four squadrons that made up the Wing on its nose, with the words, 'NEAF's Last Strike Canberra'. Finished in Dark Green and Dark Sea Grey upper surfaces over Light Aircraft Grey under surfaces, standard roundels were carried above the wings and on the fuselage sides. The underwing and fuselage serials were black and were repeated on the nosewheel doors.

Inset: Enlargement of the four Akrotiri Strike Wing squadron badges carried on the nose.

References used: p92, 'English Electric Canberra' by Ken Delve, Peter Green and John Clemons, Midland Counties Publications, 1992

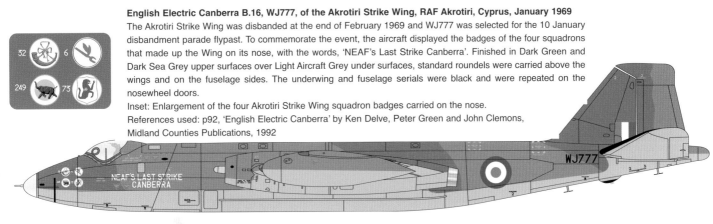

WJ777

English Electric Canberra B(I)6, WT313, of No 213 Squadron, RAF(G) Bruggen, Germany, autumn 1968

WT313 spent its entire RAF service life with No 213 Squadron, based in Germany. Finished in Dark Green and Dark Sea Grey upper surfaces over Light Aircraft Grey under surfaces, standard roundels were carried above the wings and on the fuselage sides. The underwing and fuselage serials were black. No 213 Squadron's 'Hornet' badge was carried on the fin. Note the black painted four 20mm Hispano cannon gun pack fitted over the rear bomb bay and lack of wing tip fuel tanks.

Inset: Enlargement of the No 213 Squadron 'Hornet' badge carried on the fin.

References used: p197, 'English Electric Canberra' by Ken Delve, Peter Green and John Clemons, Midland Counties Publications, 1992

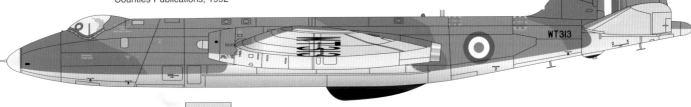

English Electric Canberra B.2, WH876, of No 85 Sqn, RAF Binbrook, November 1970

A Short Bros & Harland-built B.2, variously converted to U.10 and U.14 configuration, WH876, had already had a long service life before its time with No 85 Squadron including a stint with the Fleet Air Arm. Finished in the overall High Speed Silver scheme, it carried standard roundels above and below the wings and on the fuselage sides. The underwing and fuselage serial numbers were both in black and repeated on the nosewheel doors. No 85 Squadron's red and black checks were applied either side of the fuselage roundel with a black individual aircraft letter 'A' above the fin flash.

References used: p245, 'English Electric Canberra' by Ken Delve, Peter Green and John Clemons, Midland Counties Publications, 1992

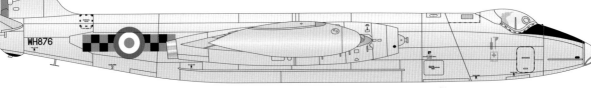

WH876

English Electric Canberra E.15, WH948, of No 98 Squadron, RAF Cottesmore, September 1972

Having previously been converted from B.6 to B.15 standard, WH948 was further modified up to E.15 standard with a specialised electronic equipment installation. Finished in Dark Green and Dark Sea Grey upper surfaces over Light Aircraft Grey under surfaces, standard roundels were carried above the wings and on the fuselage sides. The underwing and fuselage serial number was in black and repeated on the nosewheel doors. The No 98 Sqn 'Cerberus' was carried on the fin and repeated as the squadron badge on the nose, flanked by white 'zig-zags' on a red bar. Note the red engine intake 'bullets'.

Inset: Enlargement of the No 98 Squadron badge flanked by white 'zig-zags' on a red bar, carried on the nose
References used: p201, 'English Electric Canberra' by Ken Delve, Peter Green and John Clemons, Midland Counties Publications, 1992

WH948

English Electric Canberra T.4, WE188, of No 56 Squadron, RAF Akrotiri, Cyprus, early 1970s
No 56 was a English Electric Lightning F.3 equipped fighter squadron, which operated several Canberra T.4s in its Target Facilities Flight, including WE188 illustrated here. Finished in overall Light Aircraft Grey with a black anti-glare panel, standard roundels were carried above the wings and on the fuselage sides. The underwing and fuselage serials were black and were repeated on the nosewheel doors. No 56 Squadron's 'Phoenix' marking was carried on the fin and the nose, the one on the nose flanked by the squadron's red and white checks.
Inset: Enlargement of the 56 Squadron badge carried on the nose and the fin.
References used: p129, 'English Electric Canberra' by Ken Delve, Peter Green and John Clemons, Midland Counties Publications, 1992

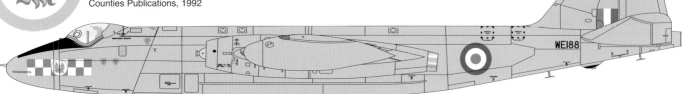

WE188

English Electric Canberra B.2, WK116, of No 100 Squadron, RAF West Raynham, 1973
A Handley Page Victor B.2 squadron throughout most of the 1960s, No 100 reformed in February 1972 as a Special Duties unit, operating several variants of Canberra well in to 1991. WK116 was finished in the then new RAF Trainer Scheme of white fuselage upper surfaces with a black anti-glare panel, with red undersides and Light Aircraft Grey wings and tailplanes. Standard roundels were carried above the wings and on the fuselage sides. The underwing and fuselage serials were black. No 100 Squadron's 'Skull and Crossbones' marking was superimposed on blue and yellow checked panel on the fin. Note the red wing tip fuel tanks and the red individual aircraft letter 'Q' on the fin.
Inset: Enlargement of No 100 Squadron's 'Skull and Crossbones' marking carried on the fin.
References used: p250, 'English Electric Canberra' by Ken Delve, Peter Green and John Clemons, Midland Counties Publications, 1992

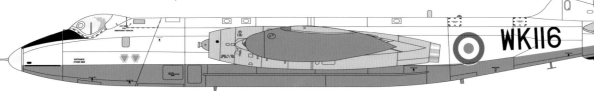

English Electric Canberra T.4, WT488, of No 360 Squadron, RAF Cottesmore, September 1973
Another specialised training unit equipped with a variety of Canberra variants, No 360 operated WT488 until it was sold to BAe in November 1981. WT488 was finished in the striking but short-lived RAF Trainer Scheme of white fuselage upper surfaces, with a black anti-glare panel, with red undersides and Light Aircraft Grey wings and tailplanes. Standard roundels were carried above the wings and on the fuselage sides. The underwing and fuselage serials were black. No other markings were carried other than a red individual aircraft letter 'Y' on the fin.

References used: p117, 'English Electric Canberra' by Ken Delve, Peter Green and John Clemons, Midland Counties Publications, 1992

English Electric Canberra T.4, WJ880, of No 100 Squadron, RAF West Raynham, 1974
As with most 'operational' Canberra squadrons, No 100 kept a T.4 on strength for pilot continuation training. WJ880, finished in overall Light Aircraft Grey with a black anti-glare panel, also carried Day-Glo fluorescent orange stripes on the nose, rear fuselage and fin. Standard roundels were carried above the wings and on the fuselage sides. The underwing and fuselage serials were black and were repeated on the nosewheel doors. No 100 Squadron's 'Skull and Crossbones' marking was carried on the fin.

Inset: Enlargement of No 100 Squadron's 'Skull and Crossbones' marking on the fin.

References used: p135, 'English Electric Canberra' by Ken Delve, Peter Green and John Clemons, Midland Counties Publications, 1992

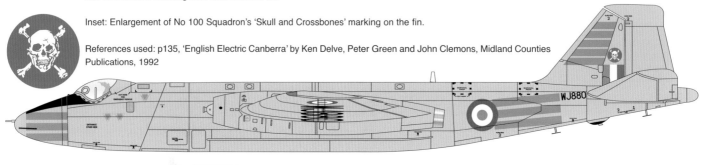

WJ880

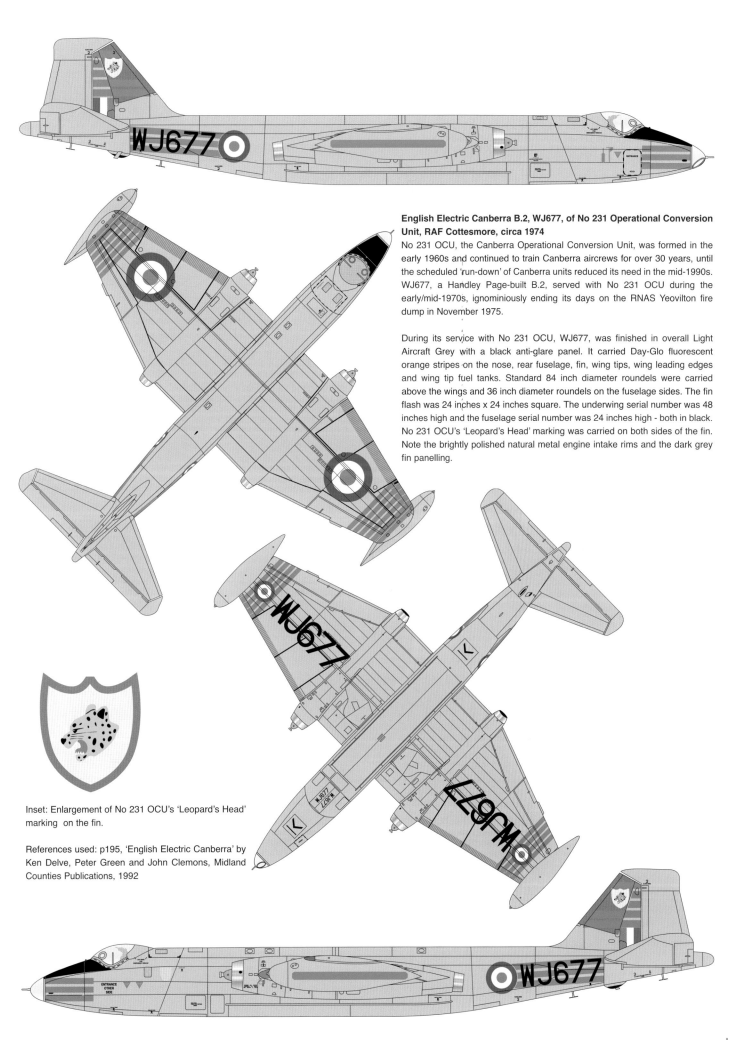

English Electric Canberra B.2, WJ677, of No 231 Operational Conversion Unit, RAF Cottesmore, circa 1974

No 231 OCU, the Canberra Operational Conversion Unit, was formed in the early 1960s and continued to train Canberra aircrews for over 30 years, until the scheduled 'run-down' of Canberra units reduced its need in the mid-1990s. WJ677, a Handley Page-built B.2, served with No 231 OCU during the early/mid-1970s, ignominiously ending its days on the RNAS Yeovilton fire dump in November 1975.

During its service with No 231 OCU, WJ677, was finished in overall Light Aircraft Grey with a black anti-glare panel. It carried Day-Glo fluorescent orange stripes on the nose, rear fuselage, fin, wing tips, wing leading edges and wing tip fuel tanks. Standard 84 inch diameter roundels were carried above the wings and 36 inch diameter roundels on the fuselage sides. The fin flash was 24 inches x 24 inches square. The underwing serial number was 48 inches high and the fuselage serial number was 24 inches high - both in black. No 231 OCU's 'Leopard's Head' marking was carried on both sides of the fin. Note the brightly polished natural metal engine intake rims and the dark grey fin panelling.

Inset: Enlargement of No 231 OCU's 'Leopard's Head' marking on the fin.

References used: p195, 'English Electric Canberra' by Ken Delve, Peter Green and John Clemons, Midland Counties Publications, 1992

English Electric Canberra B.6(Mod), WT305, of No 51 Squadron, RAF Wyton, April 1976

One of a batch of six aircraft built by English Electric, as replacements for diverted airframes, WT305 was used as a test bed for various projects including Infra-Red Sensor and flight trials for the Royal Radar Establishment, (RRE). Operated by No 51 Sqn, it was finished in Dark Green and Dark Sea Grey upper surfaces over Light Aircraft Grey under surfaces. Low visibility red/blue roundels were carried above the wings and on the fuselage sides. The underwing and fuselage serials were black, as was the individual aircraft letter 'X' on the nosewheel doors. Note the ESM 'dustbin' behind the cockpit and the strake on the forward fuselage side which may have been part of the 'Project Zabra' fit.

References used: p49, 'English Electric Canberra' by Ken Delve, Peter Green and John Clemons, Midland Counties Publications, 1992

X

English Electric Canberra TT.18, WJ721, of No 7 Squadron, RAF St Mawgan, April 1976

Built as a B.2, WJ721 was converted to TT.18 in 1968 and served with the Royal Navy's Fleet Requirements Unit, (FRU), before transferring back to the RAF with No 7 Squadron. Finished in Dark Green and Dark Sea Grey upper surfaces, the under surfaces were yellow with broad black diagonal stripes. Low visibility red/blue roundels were carried above the wings and on the fuselage sides. The underwing and fuselage serials were black, repeated on the nosewheel doors. The 'last two' in the form of a red individual aircraft number was carried on the fin. The No 7 Squadron badge, the seven stars of the constellation 'Ursa Major' on a blue disc was also carried on the fin. Note the Rushton target-towing winch and 'target' on the port pylon.

Inset: Enlargement of No 7 Sqn's 'Ursa Major' marking on the fin.

References used: p470, 'Thirty Years of Canberras' by Terry Brown, Airfix Magazine, Gresham Books, May 1980

WJ721

English Electric Canberra T.17, WK102, of No 360 Squadron, RAF Cottesmore, late 1970s

WK102 was one of twenty-four Canberra B.2s converted to T.17 standard in 1967, after serving briefly as a 'straight' bomber with the RNZAF amongst other RAF units. Operated by No 360 Sqn, in the Electronic Counter Measures (ECM) training role, it was finished in matt Dark Green and Dark Sea Grey upper surfaces over Light Aircraft Grey under surfaces. Low visibility red/blue roundels were carried above the wings and on the fuselage sides. The underwing and fuselage serials were black, repeated on the nosewheel doors. A white individual aircraft letter 'A' was carried on the fin together with the No 360 Sqn badge of a moth superimposed over a trident.

Inset: Enlargement of No 360 Squadron's 'Moth and Trident' marking on the fin.

References used: p138, 'English Electric Canberra' by Ken Delve, Peter Green and John Clemons, Midland Counties Publications, 1992

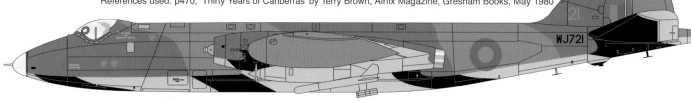

WK102

English Electric Canberra T.19, WJ975, of No 100 Squadron, RAF Marham, October 1979

Starting life as an English Electric-built T.4, WJ975 was progressively modified, first in to a T.11 with its distinctive, pointed nose housing the AI radar, and then with the radar removed, into T.19 configuration, in which form it served with No 100 Sqn in the late 1970s. Finished in the matt Dark Green and Dark Sea Grey upper surfaces over Light Aircraft Grey under surfaces scheme, low visibility red/blue roundels were carried above the wings and on the fuselage sides. The underwing and fuselage serials were black and there was a black individual aircraft letter 'S' on the fin together with the No 100 Sqn 'Skull and Crossbones' marking superimposed on blue and yellow checked panel.

Inset: Enlargement of No 100 Squadron's 'Skull and Crossbones' marking on the fin.

References used: p136, 'English Electric Canberra' by Ken Delve, Peter Green and John Clemons, Midland Counties Publications, 1992

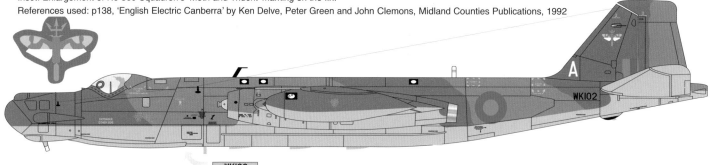

English Electric Canberra E.15, WH972, of No 100 Squadron, RAF Wyton, early 1980s

Starting life as an Short Bros-built B.6, WH972 was first modified upto the improved bomber B.15 standard and then later to the electronic warfare E.15 standard, in which guise it served with No 100 Sqn, until it crashed on approach to RAF Kinloss in June 1990. Finished in matt Dark Green and Dark Sea Grey upper surfaces over Light Aircraft Grey, low visibility red/blue roundels were carried above the wings and on the fuselage sides. The underwing and fuselage serials were black and repeated on the nosewheel doors. White code letters were positioned on either side of the fuselage roundel - 'C' for No 100 Sqn and 'M' as the individual aircraft letter. The No 100's 'Skull and Crossbones' marking superimposed on blue and yellow checked panel was carried on the fin.

Inset: Enlargement of No 100 Squadron's 'Skull and Crossbones' marking on the fin.

References used: p137, 'English Electric Canberra' by Ken Delve, Peter Green and John Clemons, Midland Counties Publications, 1992

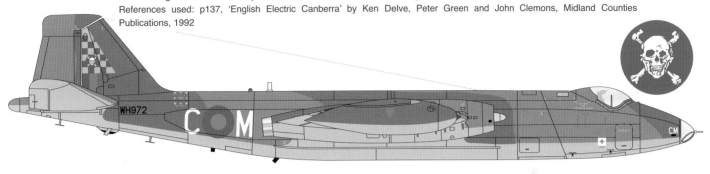

WH972

English Electric Canberra B.15, WH960, of No 2 School of Technical Training, (SoTT), RAF Cosford, May 1982

Serving with No 32 Sqn as part of the Akrotiri Strike Wing during the late 1960s/early 1970s, WH960 was retired as a ground instructional airframe in 1973 with the serial 8344M. Still sporting its No 32 Sqn black and white diagonal bars either side of the fuselage roundel and its 'operational' serial number, WH960 was finished in Dark Green and Dark Sea Grey upper surfaces over High Speed Silver under surfaces. Standard roundels were carried above the wings and on the fuselage sides. The underwing and fuselage serials were black and were repeated on the nosewheel doors. There was a red individual aircraft letter 'A' on the fin above a white or silver rectangle.

References used: p200, 'English Electric Canberra' by Ken Delve, Peter Green and John Clemons, Midland Counties Publications, 1992

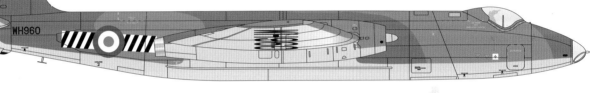

English Electric Canberra T.4, WJ879, of No 231 Operational Conversion Unit, RAF Wyton, May 1990

WJ879 spent a large proportion of its service life in the Station Flights of most of the UK Canberra bases before finally settling in with 231 OCU. By the early 1990s it was finished in the matt Dark Green and Dark Sea Grey upper surfaces over Light Aircraft Grey under surfaces scheme, with low visibility red/blue roundels above *and* below the wings and on the fuselage sides. No underwing serials were carried but the fuselage serials were black and repeated on the nosewheel doors. Black code letters 'BH' were carried on the fin together with the 231 OCU 'Leopard' badge on a white disc.

Inset: Enlargement of the 231 OCU 'Leopard' badge on the fin.

References used: p196, 'English Electric Canberra' by Ken Delve, Peter Green and John Clemons, Midland Counties Publications, 1992

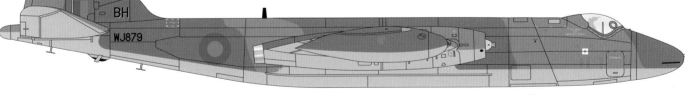

English Electric Canberra B.2, WK128, of the Royal Aircraft Establishment, (RAE), Llanbedr, May 1990

WK128 spent its entire life as a research and development airframe, mainly with the Royal Radar Establishment, acting as a jamming aircraft for 'window' launching trials through to AQM-37A 'Stiletto' launch trials, finally serving with the Royal Aircraft Establishment and Flight Refuelling Ltd at Llanbedr. Finished in the distinctive RAE 'Raspberry Ripple' Scheme, of red, white and blue wing and fuselage upper surfaces, with yellow and black diagonal striped under surfaces, standard roundels were carried above the wings and on the fuselage sides, thinly outlined in white. The underwing serials were black and the fuselage serials were white. The 'Royal Aircraft Establishment' logo was carried high up on the forward fuselage with the RAE 'Coat of Arms' lower down on the nose.

Inset: Enlargement of the RAE 'Coat of Arms' on the nose.

References used: p208, 'English Electric Canberra' by Ken Delve, Peter Green and John Clemons, Midland Counties Publications, 1992

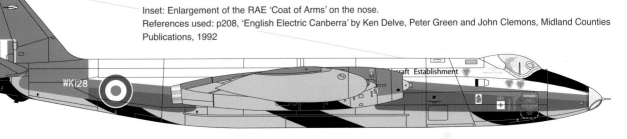

English Electric Canberra TT.18, WJ717, '841' of the Fleet Requirements and Air Direction Training Unit, (FRADTU), RNAS Yeovilton, June 1977

Operated by Airworks Services Ltd, flying target facilities duties, originally as No 776 Fleet Requirements Unit based at Hurn, the unit moved to Yeovilton and changed its name in the early 1970s to the Fleet Requirements and Air Direction Training Unit, (FRADTU). One of several B.2/TT.18 conversions on FRADTU's inventory, WJ717 was finished in Light Aircraft Grey upper surfaces with a black anti-glare panel, it had a broad red band around the rear fuselage and yellow and black diagonal striped under surfaces. Standard roundels were carried above the wings and on the fuselage sides. The underwing and fuselage serials were black as was the 'ROYAL NAVY' legend. The individual aircraft number '841' was white on a black rectangle on the nose. Note the 776 FRU 'Penguin' unit crest on the fin. References used: p120, 'English Electric Canberra' by Ken Delve, Peter Green and John Clemons, Midland Counties Publications, 1992

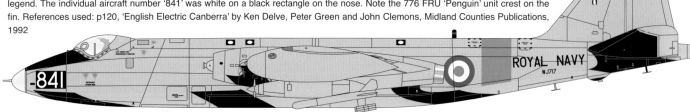

English Electric Canberra TT.18, WK123, '840' of the Fleet Requirements and Air Direction Unit, (FRADU), RNAS Yeovilton, early 1980s

WK123 served for many years with the RRE, A&AEE before being transferred to the Royal Navy as a target tug in 1969. Operated by Airworks Services Ltd, it is illustrated as it looked after the unit had dropped the word 'Training' in its original FRADTU title. Finished in Light Aircraft Grey upper surfaces with a black anti-glare panel, it carried a broad yellow band around the rear fuselage. The under surfaces carried yellow and black diagonal strips. Standard roundels were carried above the wings and on the fuselage sides. The underwing and fuselage serials were black as was the 'ROYAL NAVY' legend. The individual aircraft number '840' was white on a black rectangle on the nose.

References used: Private photo archives

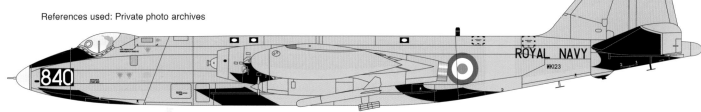

English Electric Canberra T.4, WJ874, '858' of the Fleet Requirements and Air Direction Unit, (FRADU), RAF Brize Norton, June 1985

WJ874 was transferred to the Royal Navy in November 1969, and served with the Fleet Requirements Unit, operating out of Brize Norton, before being returned to RAF charge in April 1986, with 231 OCU. Finished overall in Light Aircraft Grey with a black anti-glare panel, it carried Day-Glo fluorescent orange stripes on the nose, rear fuselage, fin, wing tips, wing leading edges and wing tip fuel tanks. Standard roundels were carried above *and* below the wings and on the fuselage sides. The underwing and fuselage serials were black as was the 'ROYAL NAVY' legend. The individual aircraft number '858' was in black on the nose.

References used: p118, 'English Electric Canberra' by Ken Delve, Peter Green and John Clemons, Midland Counties Publications, 1992

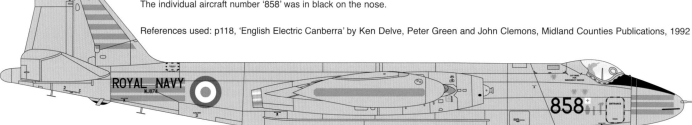

English Electric Canberra T.22, WH780, '853' of the Fleet Requirements and Air Direction Unit, (FRADU), RNAS Yeovilton, early 1985

WH780 was originally built as a PR.7. It was converted to T.22 standards in early 1974 and transferred to Royal Navy charge, serving with the FRADU at RNAS Yeovilton until September 1985, when it became the last T.22 to serve with the unit. Finished overall in Light Aircraft Grey with a black anti-glare panel, it carried red 'Trainer Bands' around the wings and rear fuselage. Standard roundels were carried above *and* below the wings and on the fuselage sides. The underwing and fuselage serials were black as was the 'ROYAL NAVY' legend. The individual aircraft number '853' was in black on the nose.

References used: p121, 'English Electric Canberra' by Ken Delve, Peter Green and John Clemons, Midland Counties Publications, 1992

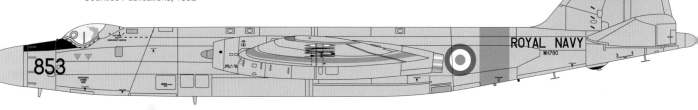

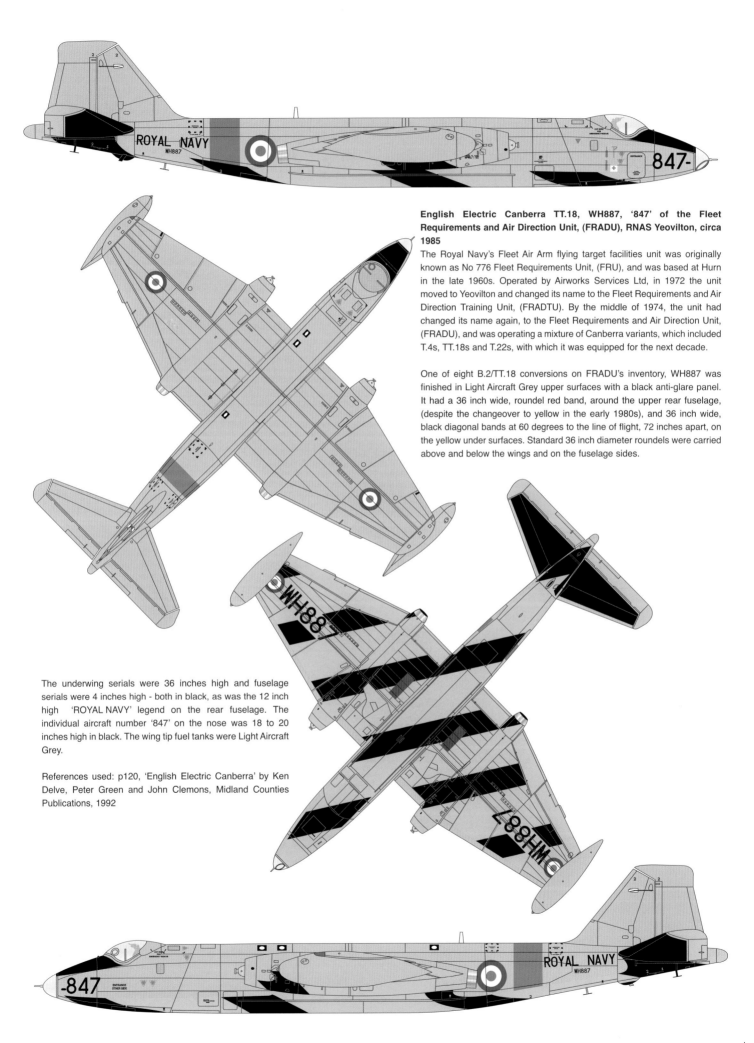

English Electric Canberra TT.18, WH887, '847' of the Fleet Requirements and Air Direction Unit, (FRADU), RNAS Yeovilton, circa 1985

The Royal Navy's Fleet Air Arm flying target facilities unit was originally known as No 776 Fleet Requirements Unit, (FRU), and was based at Hurn in the late 1960s. Operated by Airworks Services Ltd, in 1972 the unit moved to Yeovilton and changed its name to the Fleet Requirements and Air Direction Training Unit, (FRADTU). By the middle of 1974, the unit had changed its name again, to the Fleet Requirements and Air Direction Unit, (FRADU), and was operating a mixture of Canberra variants, which included T.4s, TT.18s and T.22s, with which it was equipped for the next decade.

One of eight B.2/TT.18 conversions on FRADU's inventory, WH887 was finished in Light Aircraft Grey upper surfaces with a black anti-glare panel. It had a 36 inch wide, roundel red band, around the upper rear fuselage, (despite the changeover to yellow in the early 1980s), and 36 inch wide, black diagonal bands at 60 degrees to the line of flight, 72 inches apart, on the yellow under surfaces. Standard 36 inch diameter roundels were carried above and below the wings and on the fuselage sides.

The underwing serials were 36 inches high and fuselage serials were 4 inches high - both in black, as was the 12 inch high 'ROYAL NAVY' legend on the rear fuselage. The individual aircraft number '847' on the nose was 18 to 20 inches high in black. The wing tip fuel tanks were Light Aircraft Grey.

References used: p120, 'English Electric Canberra' by Ken Delve, Peter Green and John Clemons, Midland Counties Publications, 1992

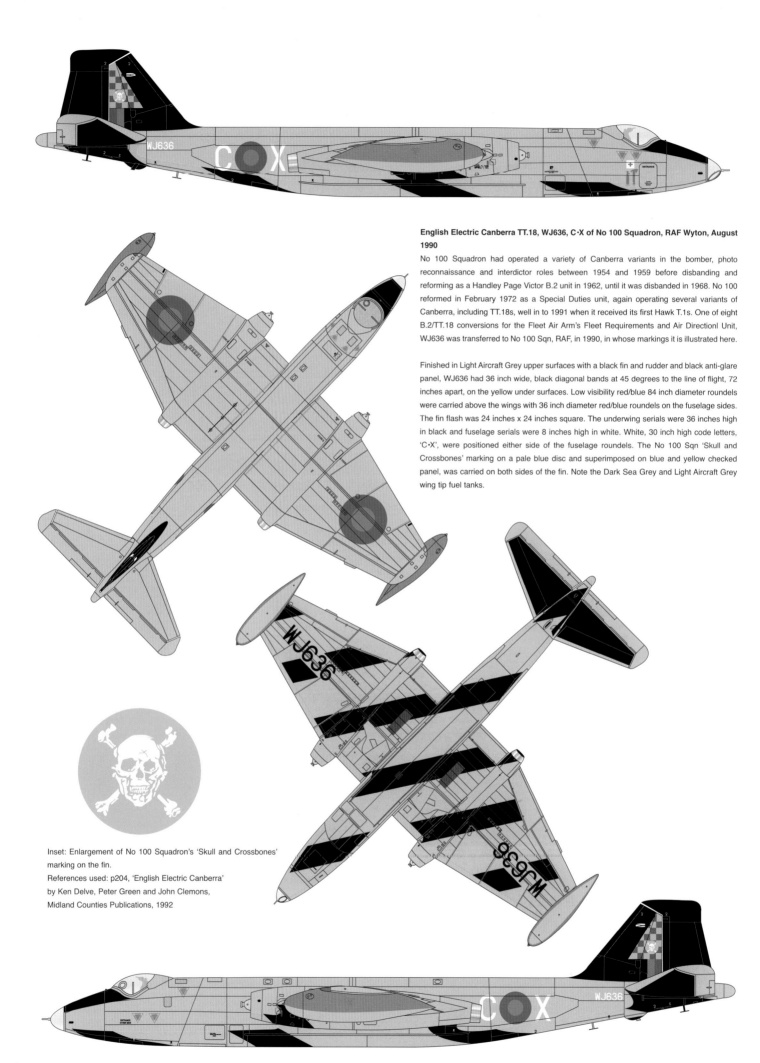

English Electric Canberra TT.18, WJ636, C·X of No 100 Squadron, RAF Wyton, August 1990

No 100 Squadron had operated a variety of Canberra variants in the bomber, photo reconnaissance and interdictor roles between 1954 and 1959 before disbanding and reforming as a Handley Page Victor B.2 unit in 1962, until it was disbanded in 1968. No 100 reformed in February 1972 as a Special Duties unit, again operating several variants of Canberra, including TT.18s, well in to 1991 when it received its first Hawk T.1s. One of eight B.2/TT.18 conversions for the Fleet Air Arm's Fleet Requirements and Air Directionl Unit, WJ636 was transferred to No 100 Sqn, RAF, in 1990, in whose markings it is illustrated here.

Finished in Light Aircraft Grey upper surfaces with a black fin and rudder and black anti-glare panel, WJ636 had 36 inch wide, black diagonal bands at 45 degrees to the line of flight, 72 inches apart, on the yellow under surfaces. Low visibility red/blue 84 inch diameter roundels were carried above the wings with 36 inch diameter red/blue roundels on the fuselage sides. The fin flash was 24 inches x 24 inches square. The underwing serials were 36 inches high in black and fuselage serials were 8 inches high in white. White, 30 inch high code letters, 'C·X', were positioned either side of the fuselage roundels. The No 100 Sqn 'Skull and Crossbones' marking on a pale blue disc and superimposed on blue and yellow checked panel, was carried on both sides of the fin. Note the Dark Sea Grey and Light Aircraft Grey wing tip fuel tanks.

Inset: Enlargement of No 100 Squadron's 'Skull and Crossbones' marking on the fin.
References used: p204, 'English Electric Canberra' by Ken Delve, Peter Green and John Clemons, Midland Counties Publications, 1992

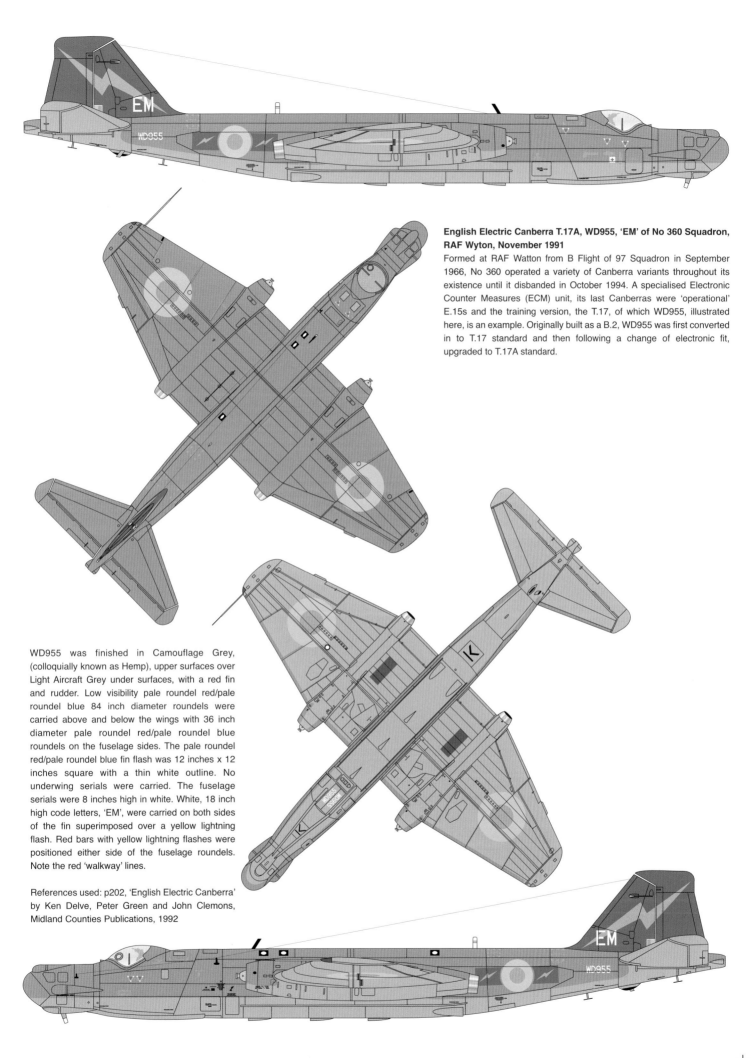

English Electric Canberra T.17A, WD955, 'EM' of No 360 Squadron, RAF Wyton, November 1991

Formed at RAF Watton from B Flight of 97 Squadron in September 1966, No 360 operated a variety of Canberra variants throughout its existence until it disbanded in October 1994. A specialised Electronic Counter Measures (ECM) unit, its last Canberras were 'operational' E.15s and the training version, the T.17, of which WD955, illustrated here, is an example. Originally built as a B.2, WD955 was first converted in to T.17 standard and then following a change of electronic fit, upgraded to T.17A standard.

WD955 was finished in Camouflage Grey, (colloquially known as Hemp), upper surfaces over Light Aircraft Grey under surfaces, with a red fin and rudder. Low visibility pale roundel red/pale roundel blue 84 inch diameter roundels were carried above and below the wings with 36 inch diameter pale roundel red/pale roundel blue roundels on the fuselage sides. The pale roundel red/pale roundel blue fin flash was 12 inches x 12 inches square with a thin white outline. No underwing serials were carried. The fuselage serials were 8 inches high in white. White, 18 inch high code letters, 'EM', were carried on both sides of the fin superimposed over a yellow lightning flash. Red bars with yellow lightning flashes were positioned either side of the fuselage roundels. Note the red 'walkway' lines.

References used: p202, 'English Electric Canberra' by Ken Delve, Peter Green and John Clemons, Midland Counties Publications, 1992

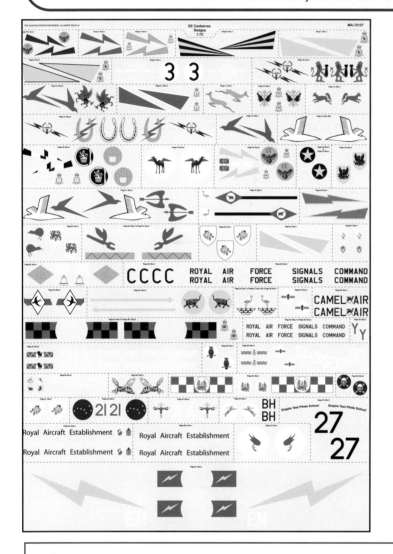